Facing The Darkness
A story of Resilience

Memoir by Rose Hylton

.

Author Rose Hylton
Cover design & pre-production Nadine Hylton-King Printed by KDP.
Independently published Copyright © 2020 Rose Hylton All rights reserved.

Acknowledgements

Firstly, I would like to thank my friend Colin Francis, for his continual support, care, and thoughtfulness throughout the entire process of the writing of my story.

I am equally grateful to my daughter Nadine, without whom, I could not have maneuvered my way through the business element of the production of this book and her unceasing encouragement for me to 'Keep going'.

Thanks to my youngest daughter Stephanie, who never judged me, whilst patiently listening to my self-doubt.

A special thanks to Mark Gunning, now deceased, who would have been proud that I had done it!

My gratitude extends to those people who contributed by offering reassurance, by proof reading and by allowing me to share my concerns over disclosing my personal story, when I needed it most: You know who you are.

Finally, I attribute thanks to you the readers, who are willing and kind enough to read the details of my testing life journey.

Sunshine and Clouds

When I was about 11, I remember my Mum pressing my hair with a steaming hot metal comb to ensure my hair was straight, less cumbersome, silky smooth – like the white girls.

Mum and Dad made sure that I spoke English properly. I was scolded if I so much as uttered a word of Patois because it was important that I fit in with the British society around us.

My parents, very much influenced by the levels of racial discrimination surrounding Caribbean people, believed that speaking proper English would distance me from the world of prejudicial behaviour. However, as I was born in England, I wasn't quite sure what I was meant to be fitting into.

From the age of 10 I surveyed a decade of immense national and international grievances: Middle East leaders placed an embargo on oil distribution to us in the West causing gross unemployment, strikes and high inflation. Feminism gained spotlight through protests leading to the passing of the Equal Pay Act in 1975.

1972 brought about the first Gay March, which led to the Sex Discrimination Act being passed three years later. Terrorist acts linked to the IRA swarmed the daily television and print media, giving rise to inherent fear amongst most people. The Falklands war arrived in the early eighties causing me to worry that my brother and his close friends might be recruited to join the armed forces.

Striding into my teenage years I recall being proud of wearing my first bell-bottomed trousers with platform shoes. I and my girlfriends sometimes referred to these shoes as, 'steppers'; because they were kinda like stepping up on a raised plinth, similar to circus artists walking on stilts. I also loved wearing mini-skirts, fashionable at the time, giving me a chance to show-off my attractive shapely legs to their fullest extent.

Listening and dancing to Disco and Motown music took precedence over the negative backdrop of my inner-city life; prompting two friends and I, to skip afternoon lessons when we learned that the Jackson 5 were staying in a Central London hotel, as part of their European tour. It seemed as if thousands of other fans had the same idea, as we quickly found ourselves surrounded by a heaving mass of squealing, babbling bodies.

I liked studying English language and literature in school and considered them my favourite subjects. I didn't mind learning about Shakespeare because he wrote about all aspects of life, like love, death, revenge, jealousy.

I related to his works because although his plays were written in early complex English, the themes were so relevant to the current world. Nevertheless, I wished that school had provided more about my own Afro - Caribbean history. The nearest I got to learning about my heritage was in our history lessons in which we were educated about slavery and the slave trade. I hated those lessons. In this subtle way, I was exposed to a derision of my ancestors, causing me to question myself as a woman of colour, particularly a woman of dark-skinned colour. You see I was led to believe that the darker one's skin colour, the less opportunities would be open to me. Our history lessons depicted that fair-skinned slave girls would be given preferential treatment by plantation owners and their henchmen, whilst darker skinned persons were used for even fewer menial roles such as toiling in the fields.

They were the ones, I was told, that were beaten, burned, hanged. The ones condemned to be the lowest of the low. As I listened to these tales, my throat tightened.

Swallowing my own saliva over and over, it took all my energy not to explode like a waterfall bursting its dam; but I couldn't because the consequences would have been too great. So, I harnessed my real feelings that could cause chaos, and meekly actioned the required lesson activity.

Splintered Lives

I Rose Diane Hylton entered the world in January 1957; no complications, natural birth; arriving with all the innocence and eagerness expected of a new-born whilst the world around me displayed dampness and cold, in tune with a typical British start to the year. Fortunately, I was born to parents who loved me and therefore received all the pomp and ceremony allotted to a first born. Two years later my brother Wilson came along. When I was twelve and he was ten years old, our sister Beverley was born.

My first home was in Smethwick, Birmingham, a three-storey house. Now don't 'get me wrong just because it was three storeys didn't mean we were rich or anything, it was the kind of house that my Dad liked. He liked big things whether that be spaces or sizes of food choices or clothing.

Our house sat amongst all the other terraced properties, side by side like mature statues, only differentiated by door colour and varied window dressings. I regarded Birmingham as a somber city. It seemed to exhibit floods of grey seeping across the sky which never seemed to go anywhere. Never got brushed away.

Inside our home a cellar sat by itself in the basement of the house. Haunting and dark it housed a world in which my Dad and his male friends and family played dominoes.

From the incessant slamming of the black and white rectangular tiles coupled with cries of 'whoa Man' or 'double deuce' followed by laughter, I assessed that they were enjoying themselves. I knew my Dad had won when his deep sonorous voice raised above everyone else's shouting 'Yes oonu can't beat dat!'

Clean bedspreads and blanket coated my large double bed giving me great comfort, fulfilling the gap in which I was frozen out by my mother.

Wearing the most glorious set of naturally black tight knit curls I was always immaculately dressed. Mum had so much going on with having to deal with managing her life as a young wife and mother, coping with having migrated to a foreign country and suffering from the loss of her own mother shortly after arriving in England; meant she didn't have the time or emotional support that I ached for.

Joy was in noticeably short supply in those days. My parents being the industrious people they were, worked hard to provide us with a good standard of living in terms of food, clothing, a roof over our heads but didn't know how to provide emotional care as they fought with each other constantly. Dad's deep loud strained voice echoed in my ears as he frequently criticized and blasted my mother. I don't hate him for that time now – but I hated it then. It forced me to protect my brother even more. I didn't want the reigns of my Dad's temper to infiltrate him. But I couldn't protect myself.

I was 7 years old when my parents decided to separate. Nobody explained anything to me, but I knew that something was different. Our Dad told my Mum that my brother was going to go with him because he was a boy and should be with him as the man. I didn't like any of that at all; it felt like an empty space had arrived in my life. I didn't understand what was going on. I just knew that one of my parents wasn't there anymore which didn't make my Mum any happier. She closed in on herself even more. To have my parents separate was a very disturbing experience because I came into the world with two of them by my side and then suddenly there was a gap. I thought it was my fault that they were not together and unbeknown to me at that time, I've spent many years making sure they stayed together.

What felt like an equally sudden shift identical to when my father left, he returned to our home within a year, with my brother in tow. Life resumed its continual cycle of shouting and berating; forcing me to become preciously protective over my brother. In not wanting him to be affected by the weight of Dad's temper, I'd tenderly hold his little hand whenever the unwelcome quarrels dashed above our heads.

Gloom saturated the air like dust particles raging aimlessly
Cursing
Squabbling
Harmony in disarray
Courting pain: they rambled.

Words flared across the room like lighted cinders
The torch of leniency denied.

A finger pointed, upholding the prison
Whilst shoulders stood in unison strong and stern as they
kicked injurious declarations into the weary room,
Each like frightened cats
Waiting to pounce if given the chance.

He paraded his strength – daring her to challenge
'Go weh fram mi' she hissed
Ruinous short breaths escape from a mouth bearing the
twist of a coiled spring
'Yu tin kyu a tap sumbaddie', he slaps in defiance.
Dark brown pupils glisten uncontrollably
Eyes bereft of beauty
Shoulders drooping – she clutches her dearest friend
The book of God, which rested neatly on her lap.
Familiar passages gave some relief.

He stood above
Casting an arena of dissatisfaction.
Bitterness slept comfortably between them
Quivering under the stare of shallow black pupils I looked
on
Querying 'What happened to their love?

Behind the walls

I was a clever child. I first surmised this when my first primary school teacher announced in assembly that I had achieved the highest score in the school's Spelling Bee, 'even the hard ones.' Beaming, she added 'Clever girl Rose. Well done, you even got the words different and stopped correct'; clapping her peach-pink hands as she spoke.

To match the impeccability of my dress, my hair was kept equally clean and oiled within an inch of its life. Yellow and red ribbons held the two plaits that hung loosely behind my ears.

One day I returned from my Birmingham primary school, George Kale with some colouring pencils that a girl in my class had willingly given to me and put them in my little school bag. I had forgotten they were there; but my parents found them and accused me of taking them without permission. There was no discussion as I was reminded to 'Never tek people tings.' At that, Dad tore into me, dragging me to the basement of our house where he used to play dominoes. Here he took off his belt and ripped it several times against my legs. I cried loudly as it fell on my back, my shins, the curve of my shoulders as I tried to move to the back of him, but the stings got harsher as he grabbed my shoulders determined to 'make sure I never did it again.'

This wasn't the first time that I had to experience an adult's mistreatment during my childhood.

George Kale school mounted almost ceremoniously, inside a fusion of residential and social housing. Sturdy and austere, it boasted a single storey of grey brick, broken intermittently by large arch windows which were too high for me to look out of when I was doing my work.

I was the type of child who followed the rules set by adults. At age seven, I trusted them, believing I had no right to object, no choice to make and no voice to be heard. I simply obeyed for fear of punishment or rejection. Could this be why I was targeted by the school caretaker within the walls of George Kale school? This perverted man pounced - with no password, no admittance letter, betraying the trust of a little girl who had no power.

He regularly placed his clammy white hands inside my pants, not caring whether it hurt or not, roaming around the inside of my pubes to get his fix. I didn't know what he was looking for, he seemed to be searching. Cruelly he made me afraid of the dark, of life, of myself and of my future. It was our secret he told me; so, I didn't tell anyone. I didn't know what to do, hence each time this man would single me out in the playground, I would just go to him and let him do whatever he wanted to with my body. I didn't scream, I didn't cry. I just let him.

Children naturally rely on adults, trusting them to direct and lead; so I adjusted myself as he swished me from one side to another to get more of a better position for his fingers to find the place he was looking for. Holding my little face upwards towards his, I was forced to stare into his. He seemed to like that, his craggy features changed, becoming more serious more set; determined to have his way.

I didn't understand why his eyes widened and why he made

low groaning sounds. He'd turn me again, telling me to move to the right, move to the left as he stuck his fingers deeper inside my innocent body. Each time, I kept my eyes closed and thought about pleasant things; like my cosy bed in my room at home or combing my dolly's hair - Until it was over.

Abuse they call it

But not so to you

Oh no

Pleasure was the name of your game

Illicit pleasure with no question asked of me

Charging into my childhood veins

Seeking no permission

Just playing out your own desires

On the body of mine

Cruel and treacherous you gained access

Like a slow worm and snake – skunk-like

Leaving trails of smell and obscenities

Driving your poison into my little self

Pure and simple you exhausted yourself

Taking power and control

Taking pleasure

Where there was an unknown of such things

I was so young

And you were not.

You pedophilic soul.

19

Relaxation, Rules and Regulations

Also, at that time my insatiable appetite for reading increased. I especially followed the exploits of 'The secret seven' and 'The Famous Five' books by Enid Blyton; discovering and enjoying the escapades that the group of children would get into. It was a means of removing myself from the humdrum, noisy, stern atmosphere of my home life. I was about 10 when I discovered these books, I'm not sure how or whether someone introduced them to me but nevertheless enjoyment was to be had from each one.

I devoured the adventures of 'Heidi', written by Johanna Spyri. Heidi was an orphan sent to live with a grumpy old man, her grandfather, in the mountains of Switzerland. Here she grew into a caring, adventurous individual, who fostered my interest in a world that was distinctly different from the one in which I lived. Nothing mattered but the scene in which I was involved. Like a warm blanket, the characters sat in contrast to my inner world of unsettledness, despair, and pain. I suppose it was from then that I acquired a great love of literature, which I still have to this day. Similar to 'Heidi', Blyton's settings were also different to the inner-city location where I was living at the time; rather, they portrayed countryside places, boasting English coastlines and green elements of Dorset. There wasn't any shouting amongst parents, in fact the main characters in the stories, focused on outdoor exploits - away from parents.

My attention on these types of books slackened off as I moved into my teenage years, making way for fashion and music magazines. Sitting cross-legged on my bed, devouring the problem pages, to the radio sounds of Tamala Motown was one of my favourite pastimes.

My new environment at South Haringey Primary school introduced me to some wonderful friendships that have stood the test of time by remaining as positive constants in my life today. In contrast I also encountered 'The Ruler', a system used as a punishment tool. If you had broken any school procedures, you were told to put out your hand, which you just did – and before you knew it, you would be wacked several times with the flat side of a 12-inch plastic sometimes wooden, ruler. Although I wasn't a regular recipient of this method of control, I can tell you it was so painful both at the time of being wacked, and for some time after. The sting was meant to ensure the offence was never repeated.

The 'ruler' was mostly reserved for us girls whilst the boys received 'The cane.' The cane, a long piece of rattan wood with a hook at the far end, held by the administer and applied to the students' buttocks, calves or palms of the hands.

It was used to hit the recipient for several times and as hard as the teacher felt, befit the student's mis behaviour. Common reasons being talking in class, not finishing homework, mistakes made with classwork, fighting and truancy. It wasn't unusual to see boys leaving the Head teacher's room rubbing their behinds with the palm of their hand. Some onlookers would snigger behind their hands, loudly pronouncing, 'Oh YOU'RE in trouble'; as they watched a teacher march a student to the

Head's office for the inevitable penalty.

I was given too much responsibility at too young an age. That was the way of our family. That was the way of our culture – work hard no matter how old you were. It wasn't unusual for me to do the family shopping at nine years of age. Some of my school friends thought it was weird however, some even considered it wrong; and regarded it as being treated like a slave. It certainly felt like that - maybe the inheritance of slavery wasn't that far behind me.

It was customary for me to revisit Birmingham with my parents on a regular basis. On the upside I had the opportunity to meet-up and play with my cousins. The downside was that I was expected to help my aunts with their housework. I perceived my role as a female being hugely different to that of my brother and male cousins. At home my brother and I were both expected to fulfil household chores – him being responsible for what Dad considered 'What man must do:' like the vacuuming, emptying the bins, helping to decorate; whereas Mum insisted he learn how to cook and tidy-up in case 'Yu meet a girl and Yu will know if she narsty or not.' On the other hand, I was expected to wash, clean, and cook because I was the girl child and the oldest. It was common for me to be sent to Ridley Road market for the family groceries, with the 'push basket.' I was expected to be 'the good girl' who simply met the needs and demands of the family no matter how I was feeling.

During my Birmingham stays, I was faced with the familiar ironing wooden board, along with baskets crowded with wrinkled garments. I was expected to finish my task all in one go, whether it be: ironing, polishing furniture or vacuuming carpets.

Everything had to be done and completed in one session even if it took several hours, which it always did. I wasn't given the opportunity to work in small stages at a pace more suited to my age.

I performed my tedious duties without a word. No one helped me; the adults had other things to do – not saying that they didn't work hard, but I was young girl – a child; but not allowed to live as one. Onerous responsibility was always first. Housework and cleanliness were top of the list. I closed myself off to the sounds coming from downstairs as I stared at the piles of shirts, blouses, bedclothes, and dresses belonging to my aunts, uncles, and my younger cousins. Unlike today there were no electronic tablets or mobiles to ease the spitting sounds of the metal plate sliding across one clean item after another. Nothing to distract the increasing silence except the intermittent familiar cry of my aunt or mother from the bottom of the stairs.

'Yu finish iron yet?' Not yet I responded quickly.

I hated the sound of my Mum telling me that we would be visiting the city of my birth because I knew what was in store.

It was enough that I had to do all of that at our own home, but it felt like being farmed out as someone's slave when I had to do the same in the homes of my extended family. I was never asked, just told what to do. Taking my responsibilities seriously, I hid my resentment and worked speedily in silence - not daring to complain.

Wanting to please
Without care for herself
She lunges into action
Determined to keep the peace.

Tears form whirlpools
Within her heart
But without concern for her own needs
She is determined to please.

Her shoulders droop amidst her aching joints
Stabbing consciousness from full view
Stamping on any feelings of care
She determines to stem any tide of woe
In order to maintain the peace.

Disappointment

It was during year 12 that I experienced my first pregnancy. I was on the pill, so it was unplanned. I didn't tell any of my friends but muddled through with the daily grind of school and family life.

Unbeknown to me at the time, my head of year Miss Silvers had been keeping a close eye on me and rather unusually came into one of my classes and asked me to follow her to her room. As I did so I considered what this could be about, then reasoned it was because I hadn't completed my A level English assignment.

'Rose,' she said when we arrived in her room. Bowing her head slightly, before continuing. 'What's going on? Your English teacher tells me that several pieces of your work have not been handed in. You're a bright girl. Why aren't you doing the work?' Searching my eyes intently, she blathered on persistently.

The room felt stifling even though there was a wide-open window behind her large wooden desk, laden with exercise books and coloured folders. Looking up at her, she suddenly seemed taller than I'd recollected. I watched her waiting for an answer but instead of speech, tears rolled down my face. She looked flummoxed.

'Nothing's wrong.' I blubbered. I just haven't got round to it yet, but I will Miss.' It still doesn't answer my question', she insisted. 'Why has your work slipped?'

'The questions came thick and fast. 'You don't look okay to me. What's happening?' For some unknown reason which until this day I have yet to fathom out; she asked whether I was pregnant. The tears rolled faster with intermissions of sobs. My chin was already nestled in the base of my neck, but I managed to nod a couple of times. Putting her arms around my shoulders reassuringly, she said, 'Alright, now go back to class and I'll see you later.' Shuffling out towards the corridor I put on my plastic smile and with my head held high I re-joined my lesson.

It didn't seem that long before she again returned for me. I could see the other girls wondering what was going on, some of them calling out that very question, as I again followed her out of the room. This time she told me that she was taking me to the Head's office. 'Damn', I thought; now the Head's going to get on my case about my missing work. Bloody hell I muttered softly to myself. However, when I entered Miss Davis' office, I was blown away to see both my parents sitting in chairs to the side of Miss Davis' desk, a much more formidable one, than that of the Head of year 12.

Miss Davis was a very thin woman. As always, she was dressed in black with an austere bun tied to the top of her head. We of her school referred to ourselves as Miss Davis' girls, like an army behind a strict sergeant major, being prepared to advance on the outside world as graceful ladies.

Mum and Dad sat close to each other, disappointment screaming from their eyes. They knew, I realised. They've told them. Misty-eyed, Mum spoke first, 'Yu pregnant Rose?'

'Yes Mummy.'

'Oh, mi gosh. Why Yu go and let that happen to Yu?' she

uttered, her brown pupils flashing. 'Yu here in a good school with the teachers them for Yu to learn and look what you do?' Questions were asked but it seemed obvious that I wasn't expected to reply, so I stood in silence. The condemnation continued spilling from her lips until my Dad joined in, adding to the gloom ridden atmosphere. 'Why Yu do dis to us Rose? So much we give you and dis is what you do with it!' No one asked me what I wanted. None of them asked me how I felt. No one came near me.

I regarded myself a leper who was being reprimanded for escaping from a colony. I was still standing near the door I'd entered, inhaling the mahogany scented furniture whilst observing the four people who had all the power. Not one of them comforted me.

Trembling in my beige-brown and red uniform, I tolerated the onslaught of words that charged across the room. The two members of staff watched and listened as my parents rattled off more criticism, before Miss Davis took over to express that she was disappointed in me and that I had made a grave mistake from which I would never recover. She went on to point out that I would not amount to anything because my condition showed her that.

'You'll end up on the streets my girl', she slapped. Shaking inside, my hands clenched tightly behind my back; I determined they wouldn't see me cry. Swear words tumbled around my mind, fighting to comprehend what they were saying. Why wasn't anyone standing next to me. Had I really done something so wrong?

Miss Silvers suggested I go home with my parents even though the school day had not ended, but at this I found my voice and asked to finish my lessons for the day. The Head accepted my plea in a wearisome manner. 'Very well you may do so my girl. But remember you have a lot of work to catch up on; though I doubt you'll do it in your condition', her eyes narrowing as she lay emphasis to the final two words.

Glancing back at my parents, my lips quivering, I walked away from the cold atmosphere, feeling sorry for them. They were right. I had screwed up - I had become a great big fat lump of disappointment.

Untying a Bond

My boyfriend Daniel and I were the same age and had been dating steadily for a few months before I got pregnant. Neither of us were seeing other people and we'd often talked about being together forever. I was in love with him, and he professed to be with me too. He was the first person to learn of my pregnancy and made it clear that he wasn't ready for parenthood. He told me that if I chose to go ahead with having a child, I'd be on my own. Expecting a different outcome, his reaction was hard to digest.

I wanted that baby, but I was blocked from having it at all turns because there was no one who would support me. Consequently, I accepted that my best option was to terminate the pregnancy.

Sitting in the waiting room of the clinically white room I was asked again by the nurse, 'Are you certain you want to go through with this Miss Hylton?' She spoke politely. Although the procedure of extracting the fetus from my womb with what I termed as a small vacuum cleaner, had been explained to me in detail by my GP, I was still uncertain. I recalled the options that were given to me. Have it, terminate it or have it and give it up for adoption. Inner confusion reigned – what did I know about child rearing? Who would be there to help me? What about my future – would I have one? Looking into the kind eyes of the nurse in front of me, my moistened face nodded.

No one told me how I would feel as the egg discharged itself from my body over the coming days. I couldn't think of it as a child; but as an unwanted stream of bloody mess filtering daily from my vagina until it was gone.

No one told me that my parents would carry on their disappointment in me by moving my belongings from the room I occupied in the downstairs center of the house to one on the upper landing. I recall gaping in dismay and terror at my personal effects strewn across the empty floor; as if they too had no right to be there.

When difficulties arise
The road is blocked – nowhere to turn
Larger than life they eat and consume
Taking charge of one's mind.
Until
A new goal is formed.

Civil Servant

Working as an administrator for the Civil Service in London Euston, when I left school, was my first introduction to full-time employment. At first, I felt elated at having the opportunity to earn my own money and so, for almost a year I gathered up-to-the-minute clothes, jewelry and such like for nights out with friends, stemming the humdrum, monotony of my day-to-day slog. Scorning the repetitiveness of office work, my brain dulled as I constantly conducted a huge number of tedious tasks. Yet, it was the pull of earning my own money that made it worth-while, at least for a time.

I relished buying the clothes that I wanted and not those chosen by my Mum; not that her tastes were especially awful, it was just that my Mum's choices didn't match the modern designs I preferred. Mummy disliked the mini skirt fashion of the day and would repeatedly assert: 'Dat skirt too shart' at which I'd roll my eyes when out of her sight.

My workplace was set in timeworn premises, and my boss's looks and manner complemented the age of the building. He wore a hairy face, making him look like a senior version of Father Christmas, without the gentleness. In his opinion, school leavers were there to serve. To him this elevated his role into one more important than it was. There were no pleasantries between us, just orders. As I was the only junior in the office, it was left to me to meet his constant demands; 'Rose get me the file from the cabinet. Rose, have you done the typing for the such and such report?'; to which I complied without comment, not wanting to rock the boat. At an incredibly early age I had copied my mother, by keeping my real feelings inside and showing a fake appearance on the outside.

I toyed with leaving the job but couldn't make up my mind about what to do as an alternative. I knew I wasn't suited to clerical work but was unsure of what my future avenues could be. In the meantime, I became increasingly distressed by the domineering attitude of my office manager.

I came to resent the familiar tap, tap, tap of his mug against the corner of his desk. Never offering to make a drink for me, he would 'tap' consistently, to mean I was to get up from my desk regardless of what I was doing and go to the kitchen to make him yet another mug of tea. If I were slow in doing so, the 'tap tap' would increase in volume. 'A lovely cuppa would be nice Rose', he'd announce at least 10 times a day; or so it seemed to me anyway. Even the innocent mugs themselves begun to irritate me and one day as I clutched the handle of one of them, I nursed an overwhelming urge to throw it and its contents into his face. It was that day that I knew it was time for me to leave.

On more than one occasion I retraced how I had felt stood inside Miss Davis' office. Going over the incident in my mind again and again, I concluded that sometimes it takes the ugly mindset of others to force a change in oneself. Taking this into account, I decided to pursue something that would get me away from home as quickly as possible. I wanted to show my parents, Miss dumb Davis and my hideous boss, that I was worth far more than the contempt they had shown me. On the other hand, I recognised that their actions had prompted a major change at this point in my life. After a lot of toing and froing, I decided to pursue a course in education, with the intention of never ever treating a young person with the same derision that I had experienced.

I can barely describe to you, the elation I felt when I applied for and got accepted onto a teacher's training course in October 1976. At last, I was able to leave Mr. Hideous to his endless cups of teas. Teaching wasn't completely out of my league because of my experience as a Sunday school teacher, where I found something peaceful and rewarding in assisting children younger than myself read passages from the Bible. I had also participated in helping them with their lines when members of the church organised Christmas and Easter productions for the general congregation.

In 1980 I graduated with a Certificate in Education (Cert.Ed.) and a Bachelor of Education (B.Ed.) from the University of Southampton. I was the first member of my family to achieve a degree; motivating my cousin Lassell to follow suit. In due course, both my children and brother also successfully followed my route into the field of education – all achieving their own degrees.

Certainty must be the thought that we think.
Definite must be the words that form on our tongue
Surety of our dreams
Images will appear – as if real.
Emerging from our mind
Until unwaveringly
They manifest.
Sharper, clearer and worthier than we ever imagined.

First Time Teacher

My first teaching job after graduating was in an East London Primary school where I was responsible for a class of 31 year 6 pupils without the support of an assistant, because we didn't have teaching assistants then. I stood shiny faced and smiley whilst looking out at the gaggle of pupils before me; at the same time patting down my hair to ensure it wasn't flicking up from the rushed attention with the comb earlier that morning.

Good morning, Miss Hylton', they chirped in unison, as I scrambled in my bag for a pen - at the same time trying to focus on my morning timetable: register, coats, Maths, handwriting. At 22 years old I was still discovering how to balance the getting up in the morning, getting ready for work and being prepared with the necessary resources for each of my lessons. Sometimes this meant leaving the finishing touches to my hair to when I arrived at school.

I very quickly acclimatised to my new career and accumulated a treasure trove of incidents from working with young people. A case in point is when on a day that I was late for work, as was the protocol, my class had been collected from the playground by a colleague and accompanied to the classroom to await my arrival. When I entered my room, a couple of the children threw their arms around me, bursting into tears as they did so. Amidst sobbing and sniffling, four red eyes divulged that they thought I lived in the classroom and couldn't understand why I wasn't there that morning as usual.

The school was open plan in design so both members of staff and children were constantly aware of noises coming from various parts of the building. The open plan model gave a freedom for teachers to work collaboratively as all classes could work on noisy or quieter activities in tandem. However, one of the negative aspects was that this style didn't allow children to fully center on specific tasks without becoming distracted, and secondly, teachers had to raise their voices that much higher to gain the attention of their individual classes.

Miss Grey's class was the nearest to mine, allowing me to see my colleague shifting between desks, bending down to point out areas of work that she wanted a particular child to focus on. Teresa Grey was also a newly qualified teacher and like me, took to the busy schedule of school life with enthusiasm and pride. The children liked Teresa's sense of humour though she tended to overly hesitate when giving instructions, never quite sure of what she was about to say.

Ben was a new boy to the school. He'd recently arrived from overseas and projected an air of authority, quite royal like in one so young. His eyes dug deep into his face exposing cheekbones round and plump, matching the curve of his stomach. Ben Canteno didn't like sitting. At every opportunity he would be up and out of his chair complaining that he needed a pencil or a crayon from another child or from another corner of the room.

'Benjamin sit down. Benjamin, I've told you twice already, sit down!' Yet no matter what Teresa said, Benjamin would be up again demanding more attention.

'But Miss I need a rubber. Miss, I don't like your shoes. Who bought them for you?' Benjamin didn't like to be ignored.

'Miss Miss, My pencil jus broke.'

Occasionally, I caught Teresa's raised eyebrows as she glanced in my direction along the open white painted corridor. I felt sorry for her because I knew just how difficult it was to manage pupils who wouldn't appreciate the rules of the school and suspected Teresa was wishing that the school wasn't so 'open' when at the end of her tether, Teresa broke. Without an ounce of dithering, she shrieked. 'Benjamin Canteno - Just Ffffuck Off!'

I and several other members of staff had been a party to the build-up of this teacher's frustration and now most of the school heard her response. Ben was beside himself with delight. He bounced around the surrounding classes repeating: 'Did you hear that? She told me to Fuck off.' Did you hear that? Sheee told me to Fuck off.' Accompanied by generous giggling, small heads and bodies shook excitedly, eager to see the outcome.

The class teacher stood head in hands and red faced, as the Head sprinted towards her. 'I'll take over here Miss Grey. Please go to the staff room', the Head stated unsmilingly, at the same time grabbing hold of Teresa's arm and gently pushing her towards the exit corridor. And with that, Teresa was banished from peering eyes and incredulous gazes.

From the corner of my eye, I watched as her bell-bottomed trouser suit swished past the side of my classroom area, her upper body shaking, her hands once again covering her tear streamed face.

As a result of Teresa's unfortunate outburst, the Head teacher directed all new teachers to receive additional training in behaviour management. What is more, this incident stirred my interest towards effecting change among young people with behaviour issues.

Disillusioned, Delinquent and Disaffected

I stayed within the primary sector of education for a couple of years, before taking on the post of Senior Youth Leader in the vicinity of Finsbury Park, North London. I wanted to make a difference to the young people in the area and this was the motivation that made me go for the job. In retrospect it wasn't just a job; it was the opportunity to make changes to the lives of the young people especially the Afro-Caribbean boys that I spotted hanging about the streets in the evenings and some of them, during the daytime too during school hours.

During this period of my life, black youngsters especially black boys were often regarded by society as underachievers, lacking in ambition. I observed that they were stamped with an identity as kids of single parents, kids of absent fathers; and adolescent males who couldn't or wouldn't provide support to their children or partners.

Most of the boys I worked with were British born. Others had been sent to the UK from the West Indies and were unfamiliar with the less stern British system, which they saw as more relaxed. Some boys used the advantage of this 'looseness' to their advantage by not adhering to school ideas and rules in an attempt at personal freedom. My parents frequently told me stories of how strict it had been for them growing up in school in Jamaica, how children were 'given beaten' for the smallest of things like answering back to a teacher.

These young people drew attention from schools, the media

and sometimes their own families as - Disillusioned, delinquent, and disaffected. I however, appreciated them as spirited, eager and capable of positive achievements; given the right circumstances. I didn't know whether or not I could make a difference – but I was willing to try.

I was employed by what was then the Inner London Education Authority, specifically Islington Council to manage the running of the YMCA Youth Centre (hereafter referred to as the YM). I was responsible for the advertising of staff, and the arranging of the right activities for local youngsters aged between 13 and 17. I had to think of where to get the staff from and this came about because I was living in the area anyway and so knew some people who could offer their services. I initially focused on setting up music workshops. Members of a local band were happy to share their talents as musicians, echoing my desire to help the youths gain something from what they were interested in.

Martin was the most vocal of the group, always with a smile across his face. Tall and slim who engaged effortlessly into the atmosphere of the YM, easily swinging into gear on the evenings that it was open. Raymond, less exuberant than Martin was the band's lead singer. Paget, the most reserved member of the band didn't say very much unless the conversation was directly levelled towards him. There was a continuous sense of camaraderie amongst these men as they challenged themselves to develop new ways of laying down tracks for the young people they worked with. Paget, tall, dark and good-looking, oozed patience, and an air of complete composure. He was the kind of person who didn't show his emotions which left many of us wondering what he was thinking.

Finsbury Park was a busy multi-cultural area and the YM sat amongst concrete flats and run-down houses. The area had limited green space except for the 115-acre public park, situated between the Manor House and Finsbury Park Tube station. Many of the attendees of the Youth Centre came from single parent households, some never having met their fathers, failing miserably in school and were more interested in sports and music than the academic aspects of education. Most perceived their secondary schools as restraining, in which they felt trapped. Having limited outdoor space added to their feelings of confinement.

William Brown was the council representative with whom I regularly met to discuss the best way to support the interests of these local youngsters. Much as I wanted to ignite their interest in literacy and Maths, most of them preferred more physical activities such as playing football or pool or getting involved in the music workshops.

A short stocky individual originating from Barbados, William walked with a stoop, enticing the more confident boys to tap him on the shoulders as they passed him by. Good manners and respect stopped them from patting him on the head like a stray dog. Brown wore a continual frown. He incessantly reminded me that his hands were tied whenever I requested new equipment, his thoughts constantly on budgetary constraints. My determination never wavered though. I wanted the best equipment and layout for the club because in my opinion the youngsters deserved better, not the dated ripped armchairs, the less than sturdy wooden tables and the dirty shred bare carpeting throughout the main corridors. I didn't like the plain walls intermittently dabbed with paper notices or the untidy felt tipped scrawls bearing an assortment of names. Overly concerning myself with how to achieve my vision of brand-new furniture, décor, drum kits, guitars, keyboards, office equipment; I often lay awake at night rehearsing the argument I would give to William to persuade him of my choices.

My spine forgot to straighten as I lay slumped and saddled by catalogues of every description. My home and workplace accumulated a mass of papers and accounting, as I worked out a way, to get the obligatory supplies needed for the successful running of a youth facility. I argued for the Centre to be closed for three weeks, for the purpose of refurbishment and time to secure adequate equipment. William disagreed.

'Two,' he asserted sternly. Staring me down, while adjusting his glasses to ensure I was in eye shot when announcing that his decision was final. 'Have the figures changed?' he added.

'Only slightly'.

William tried hard not to budge, but I was equally determined and handed him a new set of figures. Rubbing his chin in contemplation he responded by reporting that his senior management were against my decision to shut the club at all, let alone for three weeks. This was going to take more convincing I realised. 'Another coffee William?' I suggested.

Pointing to an end column, I expressed that the figures were not too high. Costs of musical and sporting equipment were not cheap and that my research had thrown up the best solutions to the re-opening of this project. 'Why should these kids be given second- class stuff all the time William?' I argued, leaving him no room to interject. 'Here is an opportunity to provide something of value to them, inspiring them to value themselves. If we treat them as if they deserve the best of things, then surely this goes someway in showing them their own self-value. Don't you agree Will?'

A sigh of exasperation escaped from his lips while lacing his fingers behind his head. I smiled at this posture, noted his dilemma but ascertained that I'd won! 'Don't let me down.' he said.

In February 1983 following a temporary closure of three weeks, I re-opened the YMCA Youth Club accommodating an array of the brand-new supplies I fought hard to obtain.

Riots

I was still working at the YM at the time of the Broadwater Farm riots. These riots were a part of a series of riots that hit the UK from 1981 to 1985. Broadwater Farm is an estate in Tottenham North London. A close friend of mine lived on the estate, often referred to as 'The Farm', so I was familiar with the concrete towers connected by dense narrow walkways.

My visits always manifested a rapid heart rate as I entered the parking zone and then the urine infected lift. Rising unsteadily up to my friend's flat I would repeatedly make a point of saying 'Hi' to whomever I shared the lift with, secretly hoping they would be a safe companion. Sometimes my greeting would be acknowledged with a 'Hi or Hello' back, at other times a mere grunt or a tense silence.

The 'Farm' was built in the late sixties and contained more than 1000 flats, providing social housing for more than 3000 people. By the mid-eighties, poor investment led to the estate's deterioration and a warren of crime and dissatisfaction. The black youth at the time were agitated at the unrelenting racism they experienced from all sectors of society. The job market was discriminatory, the housing market was discriminatory, the education system was discriminatory, the law system was discriminatory, especially the SUS Law.

This law authorized police to arrest and punish suspected persons they deemed loitering in public places with criminal intent. There did not have to be any actual proof, just suspicion of intent. As a result, many black youths including some of my friends were exposed to being stopped and searched in their cars or whilst simply going about their daily business, for no purpose but to intimidate and cause affray.

The Broadwater Farm riot was sparked by the shooting of the mother of Michael Groce by police in the London borough of Lambeth. Tension already high amongst the black community from this act and earlier riots in Handsworth, Birmingham, Moss side, Manchester and Toxteth, Liverpool reached new heights when Floyd Jarrett, a young black man who lived about a mile away from the Broadwater Farm estate, was arrested and charged with theft and assault. He was later acquitted of both charges.

Later that day, the police decided to search the house of Floyd's mother, Cynthia. During the search, 49-year-old Cynthia Jarrett collapsed and died of a heart attack. A demonstration gathered outside Tottenham police station in the early hours of the next morning, escalating into violence between police and some members of the local community - centering on 'the Farm.'

The rioters assembled barricades, set fire to cars, and threw bricks, petrol bombs and other projectiles at police, making effective use of the raised walkways on the estate. Regrettably, a police officer lost his life during this acute civil unrest.

Three men were charged and sentenced to life imprisonment, one of whom was a pleasant young lad who regularly attended the YM Youth Club where I worked. I remember his infectious smile and willingness to participate in the music workshops. He and his friends never failed to nod respectfully whenever they saw me. He and the two defendants convicted for the killing of the police officer, were eventually cleared by a court of appeal when an ESDA (electrostatic detection device), demonstrated that police transcripts of interrogations had been tampered with. There was no other evidence of their alleged criminal act.

Generations of young black men
Live in a world that doesn't respect them.
Torn up inside from patrol car hate
Some unleashed their anger on The Broadwater Farm
estate.

Cars upturned and petrol bombs thrown
Seething batons met persons unknown
Anger tripped into the final stage
When the death of an officer finished the outrage.

Who was right?
And who was wrong?
People asked when the man was gone.
Does the answer matter at all?
When respect for life is believed too small.

Wedding Bliss

Jen sat with me on the sofa, her short curly black hair framing her blemish-free dark skin. Giving me sideview glances she sat still, observing my contoured features. I on the other hand was too deep in thought to notice - Was I sure? Was this what I wanted? Jennifer looked at me many times, before letting me know what she was thinking.

'Are you sure you want to go ahead? You don't have to go through it she echoed for the fourth time. 'If You're not sure it's okay. People will get over it.' I vigorously shook my head from side to side, letting her know that I intended to go ahead. 'Everything's prepared', I stated sharply, having scanned the creaseless outfits hung neatly on the outside door of my wardrobe.

I was twenty-seven years old when I got married to Paget King. My chief bridesmaid Jen stayed with me the night before my wedding, helping me prepare for my big day. We shared a two bed-roomed flat in Hornsey, North London. It was on the 10th floor seated at the corner of a terribly busy high road giving us views and endless noise of traffic and rows of brick terraced houses in the forefront.

That September morning greeted me dressed in a white satin two-piece suit; the elegant skirt and jacket, hugging my slim figure. I was happy about the knee-length and white heels high enough to strengthen my sensual look. The cloudless autumn morning echoed the joy radiated on my face. My smile widened when Jen hugged me saying, 'Girl you look amazing.' Even with the butterflies churning in my stomach, I grinned with certainty of moving into a wonderful future with a man I loved.

Last minute details to my outfit saw me dashing around the living room looking for my earrings. Much as I didn't expect to find them there, I found myself searching desperately along the navy-blue shag pile flooring in the hope that I had accidently dropped them somewhere in its midst. Casting my eyes towards the pine sideboard, I at last spotted the white rectangular small box which I knew held the pair of white pearly drop earrings, and with that I carefully hooked them into the lobes of my ears. Almost immediately, I heard the door-bell ring and muffled voices from Jen and Martin, who had arrived to drive me to the first of the two settings for my wedding day.

I entered the registry office with Martin's glowing face beside me. Holding the door open of his car and my hand at the same time, he helped me out to step towards the entrance of The Haringey Civic Centre in Wood Green, North London. It was great to be the recipient of approving smiles from close family and the few friends I had invited to this first part of my marital day. Everyone was smartly dressed but none looked as good as the 6'4 man stood ahead of me dressed in a light grey suit and white shirt, matched with white leather loafers. His carefully knotted dreadlocks reached beyond his shoulders, neatly held back into a ponytail by a white headband. Beaming as he looked down at me through black rimmed glasses, I instinctively relaxed.

The registrar who officiated our ceremony begun with a joke, expressing that it was the first time that he had married a couple where the groom's hair was longer than the bride's. Mostly to maintain a picture of enjoyment for our wedding day, the room smiled and laughed at this comment, but as Caribbean people we understood he was commenting on a hairstyle that was an aspect of the Rastafarian religion, of which Paget was one. In those days sporting dreadlocks was seen as unusual and something to be ridiculed or mocked.

Both of us eagerly answered 'Yes' when asked whether we'd take each other to be lawful wedded husband and wife; kissing to applause and cheering from our diverse generation of friends and family. I thought my heart would burst at the seams when we made our way to the Centre's gardens to take photographs. Crunchy brown leaves lay contentedly beneath the striding shoes of all our guests, as if in compliment to the idyllic atmosphere.

'Can I have the bride and bridegroom with the bride's family?' The photographer's voice could barely be heard amongst the chattering tongues surrounding me; making him use his waving arms to grab our attention. Beckoning to Paget and me, he smiled as he suggested we move towards the assembly of golden coloured trees. As we and our welcomed guests followed his instructions; I caught myself wondering what Mum, Dad and Bev were doing at that precise moment. 'Were they thinking of me? Were they even bothered?' Swallowing the surging sea of emotion that threatened to surface, I exhaled quietly and returned to the sounds of the photographer. Uttering 'Great, that's good', he gently shifted people around to secure collective and solo shots.

The saddest part of my wedding day was the fact that my parents and sister were not there. Even though other family members were there and had made a lot of effort to make my day considerably special, a part of me felt the emptiness of my parents' absence - like a gaping hole. It was a day in which I missed the familiarity of their faces, their conversation, their smiles. I imagined Dad saying something like, 'I like Yu dress', to which Mum might have replied, 'Is not a dress, is a suit, Yu caant see?'

'Of carse me can see, but it look like a dress.' My parents often bantered back and forth when discussing their opinions on something; with unconscious hilarity each would attempt to assert their rightness in any given situation.

They were the people I missed, like a child who cries when a favourite toy is taken away because the adults in charge decide the child is grown enough to let go. In the eyes of the law, I was a grown up, a proper adult; yet without my parents beside me on one of the most important days of my life, a part of me felt alone, jilted.

My parents had chosen to set up permanent residency in their home country of Jamaica, three months before my wedding. More than once Mum had intimated that she wasn't sure that Paget was right for me, but I had met my prince charming so none of her reservations took hold. I wanted the 'happy ever after dream.' Loving fairy tale stories as I did, I naturally thought this was something to strive for.

From my earliest years I was fostered on a diet of what I call the Cinderella Syndrome; the fairy tale in which the central character who after a few challenges along the way meets her handsome hero who sweeps her off her feet and ends up living 'happily ever after.' In all the books that charted this famous story, Cinderella was always depicted as a young, white, slim, beautiful blond. These images did nothing to dissuade a young black girl like me, as they were only pictures that I was exposed to. Besides that, because my Mum and Dad maintained their marriage in spite of their ups and downs, I believed even more that this would be the case for me too.

The decision for my parents to return to Jamaica was led by my Dad but Mum had to go too, because she felt it was her duty to follow her husband and she didn't want to do what some members of the West Indian tradition did, which was for him to go alone, and the wife follow on sometime later. I admired their willingness to try something new. I understood their need to return as they had left their homeland whilst in their early twenties and hadn't returned since. They had reservations about leaving their siblings but more so about leaving my brother and I, but it was something that they felt a 'pull' to do.

Over time I fathomed that the emptiness I felt that day and in the ensuing days, was in preparation for me to develop a depth of resilience that I perhaps would not have gained had they been with me. I came to understand that the void I had experienced was an opportunity to fill it with something else.

The photographer begun to wave at us again. 'Bride and Bridegroom please,' as he pointed to a beautiful corner of the gardens where with expert guidance, we dizzily and playfully posed for one shot after another.

Coated in matrimonial bliss the wedding party moved onto my childhood home, Duckett Road where we were greeted by aunts and uncles who had prepared the house for the continuation of my amazing day, a day in which I saw first-hand the extent of their love, generosity, and creativity. For instance, when I inquired where they had acquired such a large table dressed in white linen; displaying the wedding cake, place settings, glasses, flowers, and decanters of selected wines; my aunt informed me that they had unhooked the main door to the living room.

It was whilst sitting at that very table and listening to the congratulatory speeches, that my uncle interjected with what he called 'a special telegram.' It was a congratulations message from my parents - letting me know I was well and truly in their thoughts. Leaning against my new husband I shed the tears I'd held in all day.

My senior relatives continued to provide the best for me, having prepared enormous amounts of food for the additional guests due to join us for the latter part of the evening – party time! And party we did, until the early hours of the following morning.

There was a young bride in September

Who sang and danced in much splendour.

With her man on her arm

She felt electrically warm

As she soaked up a day to remember.

Unreasonable Behaviour

I'd always wanted to be a Mum, but I hadn't planned on it being so soon in my marriage. I had envisaged a world of travelling around exotic countries with my husband and working towards a headship in my teaching career. However, a smear test before we got married revealed that there was some abnormality with my cells. Further tests and a biopsy showed that I was carrying precancerous cells in my cervix. The doctor let me know that these abnormal cells needed to be destroyed by laser treatment, where medical professionals would use a small tool with an electrolyte wire loop to burn away these abnormal cells.

I remember tears settling into the grooves at the base of my neck while I listened to him advising me to have children as soon as I was able as there was a serious probability that these cells could develop into cancer and therefore reduce my chances of ever carrying a child or children. 'Any questions?' he enquired. Rubbing one of my hands over the other I looked at him and responded barely above a whisper. 'So, are you saying that if I want children, I need to consider having them now?'

'Yes', he replied gently.

Cancer, cancer - the words enveloped my thoughts like mangled train tracks. Cancer I repeated to myself as I walked out of the pristine well-ordered surgery. I could barely comprehend the precancerous bit until later when I discussed it with P. Embracing me warmly, he assured me that everything would be alright and if I got pregnant soon, then we'd deal with it.

I was nearly three months pregnant when I got married. I was five months pregnant when my husband first hit me. My world became a far cry from the one I had imagined, for out of the blue, I had moved into a world of domestic violence.

At that time, Paget and I were living in Edmonton, North London. My brother and I had sold the family home in Duckett Road shortly after my wedding and we each used our share as deposits towards our individual properties. Mum and Dad had previously sold the family home to us at a reduced price as a kind of inheritance payment, so I was able to obtain a mortgage with my share.

With the security of my job and my deposit, I was easily able to purchase our matrimonial home. Paget's income was terribly precarious being a sessional musician, but I was optimistic that this would change, and we'd meet the financial commitments required. Our three-bedroomed house was bordered on each side by equally terraced properties. Each front garden boasted its own uniqueness, ours hosting a myriad of plants, but especially my magnolia tree. It majestically took central stage; and I never tired of the sweet - perfumed scent from the pinky-white goblet shaped flowers during the spring and summer months. Identical to the other houses along the street, the large bay windows to the front suggested a long vista of respectability, interrupted only by secretive curtains. The two-storey house enjoyed a path running down the side away from the well-kept, evenly paved road. This beautiful home bore witness to my first assault.

It was Christmas eve, and I was putting the finishing touches to our Christmas meal. Turkey seasoned, tick; potatoes peeled, tick; red peas in the pot for the rice, tick; vegetables in fridge, tick; fish seasoned ready for frying, tick; apple crumble ready for baking, tick. As I was clearing and cleaning the kitchen surfaces Paget joined me in the kitchen to see what I was doing. He seemed in a good mood, so I thought I'd mention that a new year and a baby were about to happen and whether he'd thought anymore about how we were going to manage financially because my salary alone was not covering our daily needs as it was, let alone with a child on the way. I reminded him that my maternity leave would severely reduce my salary even further. With a sudden dart he reached over at me and begun dragging me backwards towards the open door. My dressing gown flew open as he continued to drag me through the hallway and up the flight of stairs. He shoved me into our bedroom – Paget always hurt me in the bedroom. Wherever I happened to be in the house, he would always haul me to the bedroom. I'm still not sure why this spot. As I was being dragged, I didn't say anything. I had frozen. When I think back on it now, I believe I was too shocked. Nothing seemed to make sense - my mind had separated itself from my body.

Instinctively I grabbed hold of the stair handrail hoping he would let me go. It wasn't until I was being punched and kicked in the bedroom that some sense of realism dawned on me. My skin crawled in terror. Was I wrong in wanting to talk about our financial situation? I heard my Mum's voice come out of me – soft, slow, not raised; 'The baby the baby' I whimpered, clutching my stomach. He didn't see me. Rage took over as he jammed his foot into my side. I took the punches to my face, to my legs, to my back, whilst my lean body curved into a fetus position, lay on the floor, my hands gripping one of the legs of the bed - my eyes firmly closed. The scent of stale hot sweat teemed from him as he continued his lashing attack. My head rocked from side to side when he paused to glare at me, eyes pinched, before resuming his assault, as if asking himself whether to continue or not - no words uttered from his lips, he answered with another wash of fists and feet.

Mrs. nice shows no anger
Mrs. nice does not blame
She goes about her business
Come sunshine, snow or rain.

Never one to cause disturbance
Mrs. nice doesn't create a scene
She learns to live in silence.
With things that are obscene.

During my pregnancy Paget arrived home with a Doberman puppy he'd got from a friend of ours. The puppy was a lovely gracious dog whom we named 'Lucky.' I had no idea he was keen on dogs but didn't question his decision and hoped he would take responsibility and give him the attention any pet needs. Initially Paget treated the puppy with reasonable care, though sometimes ignoring him and shoving him outside when Lucky irritated him. I felt so sorry for the poor little mite but being heavily pregnant and worrying about the increasing bills, I didn't feel able to get to do much about that as well except feed him.

My morning routine generally begun with me going downstairs to make breakfast and looking around for the puppy to feed him too. I didn't know quite what to do when I saw Lucky wasn't in his usual place in the kitchen. Instantly I worried about Paget's reaction when he returned from his night in the recording studio. I searched behind worktops and looked around the living room to no avail. I tell you now, that part of me was relieved and another part was filled with dread as I considered what P might do when he found Lucky missing so decided to say nothing; simultaneously I worried whether he'd killed it. I was unsure. I knew that the previous evening he'd kicked the poor thing so hard when I'd heard Lucky's cries as she was careered out into the garden. 'What could this defenseless animal have done?' I considered. Lucky wore a chestnut brown coat that matched the chestnut colour shading on her nose and paws, making it easy see her contrasted against our light pine furniture.

Not wanting to antagonise my husband in any way, I rushed back upstairs when I heard him open the front door. Hovering over the banister, I quaked at every step he took; wholeheartedly hoping Lucky had found a new and kinder owner. Contemplating that at least one of us had got away, brought me some relief.

Surprisingly, Paget was only mildly irritated when he realised Lucky had gone. Having searched the garden, he found that there was a gap in the fence where he had probably run through. Shrugging his shoulders, he reconciled that his pup had escaped to someone who had deliberately looked for an opportunity to take him for themselves or to sell on.

Whenever I experienced any small sign of reasonable behaviour from my husband, I felt hope. His response to Lucky's disappearance was a far cry from all his mammoth outbursts up to that point. I saw this reaction as progress towards a peaceful relationship.

At that juncture in my life, I believed a good marriage was one in which two people would equally share the ups and downs of daily life. I believed that harmony was a must, and that love would conquer any disagreements. I wasn't a fantasist, thinking that the two people would always agree on everything, but I imagined that things could always be worked out through discussion and negotiation. I was certain that a good marriage involved each person feeling at ease with his or herself in the relationship.

In contrast, my marriage imparted such torturous fear and resentments I had never experienced before - escalating to dizzying heights after the birth of my two daughters. My growing concern for the protection and health of my first born led me to collapse in tears as I confided to my GP about what I was experiencing at home. On his recommendation I was admitted to North Middlesex hospital a few weeks earlier than was usual, to keep us safe.

Nadine was born in April 1985 with her father beside me. The delight a baby can bring to even the most iniquitous person is quite remarkable. Paget was just as overjoyed at her entry into the world as I was. However, babies need constant care, constant attention, constant nurturing; none of which my husband provided. Nevertheless, I got on with it; driven by the love I had for her, determined she would feel as secure as possible.

In the process I was losing weight and suffering from extreme exhaustion as I singlehandedly tried to manage Nadine's feeding times, bathing, medical appointments and find time to keep up with the household tasks. On the other hand, Paget continued spending most of his time at the recording studio working on an album.

Eight months after the birth of Nadine, I was pregnant with Stephanie. I knew that it would be even harder to cope with two children and a man who took little responsibility for our care. I could barely cope with his dark moods and continual put downs, making me feel less and less confident. I encouraged him to seek counselling with me but after only two sessions he refused to attend. Here again, he'd let me down. Bloody unconcerned with the impact of his actions on us as a family made me furious. He wasn't even prepared to look at ways that may have helped us form a better relationship – not even for the kids. The mortgage company was demanding payments every month that I couldn't meet; so too the credit card company, never mind all the regular bills like gas, electricity, phone, and car payments. Paget's financial contribution was miniscule and too erratic to make any difference to the situation. I couldn't have blazing rows with him because I was too frightened of the outcome so instead, I went to stay with a friend for a couple of days, in the hope that this would ease the tension between us and give me time to think more closely about what was the best thing for me to do. Maybe we're not meant to be together? Sometimes I believed it would work out and at others it seemed an impossibility. Paget's dilemma was that he wished to promote and play his talents in music other than reggae; yet the professionals in the music industry would only entertain him as a reggae artist. I understood his disappointment at being pigeonholed solely on his Rastafarian status but then again, I also knew that I did not deserve to be the butt of his frustrations. I made the decision to walk away.

Being pregnant with a second child, I saw no option but to sell the house and separate. P didn't like that idea but could not offer a better alternative. My words wobbled and quivered as I told him that I wanted a legal separation because I felt our marriage was not working out. The air between us took on a heaviness which slithered inside him, as if lying dormant beneath a tightly closed lid.

Once the sale of the house was completed and all financial commitments settled, I was left with a cheque of a mere £45.00 to start again. Nadine, I and my unborn child were housed in a women's refuge while I badgered the local council for a permanent place for us to live, as I didn't want to remain in the refuge for any longer than was necessary. The refuge was dismally small with no outside space. All of us women were there for the same reason – hiding from the sufferance of abusive partners. This was our camaraderie, our reason for being together. We shared stories of what we had gone through, often sobbing over how on earth we'd ended up in that position. I did not like having to share a bathroom with 3 other women and children; I did not like the far cry from my well- kept home in Webber Street; but I had no choice. I had a baby growing in my belly, little money and fearful of my husband's temper.

For six weeks I tolerated the perpetual noise, the shabbiness of the shared living quarters and the scantily furnished bedroom. I remember looking down at the sheet covering the single bed and wondering what the woman before me was like? Was her life better now? Had she recovered from her injuries? Would I recover from mine?

Disappointments trampled mischievously across her soul
Daring her to feel an ounce of joy
She resisted
Weakened by the throes of the enemy
She reeled motionless into the palms of the unfamiliar
Hope is lost.

The day I was offered keys to my council flat in Finsbury Park was like no other. At last, I could lay down on a bed I'd chosen, walk on flooring that wasn't covered with old stains of who knows what; cook what I wanted in a kitchen that was mine. Believe me, despite the support the refuge had given me, I was hungry to provide a decent home for my kids.

I was still in love with P and reluctant to end my marriage, so after a few months of moving onto the Six Acres Estate, we got back together again. I wasn't prepared to give up on us and wanted the children to be part of a family unit. I promised myself that I'd do better, I would make our relationship work. What transpired was that nothing had changed except the address. I was trapped in a relationship of frustration and regret, constantly praying for an end to the exhausting turmoil. I wanted to escape from the nightmare I found myself in; yet still loving my husband I didn't know how I could make myself different so that he wouldn't keep hurting me. I wasn't a large built woman, a size 14, but with the stress of money worries and learning the ropes as a new Mum, my weight plummeted to a size 10 and below. I suffered insomniac episodes, panic attacks and constant headaches. It was like sacrificing my well-being to a belief that this was what marriages were about.

Day after day I would pray to God for some sign, some way out. There were only two questions in my mind – Should I stay, or should I go? And if I did leave, where was I to go to? I desperately wanted a cheerful home life for myself and our children, but time kept conveying that this was not going to be the case. In short, I became more and more edgy as I noticed how sharp-tongued Paget would get with our daughters, whenever he was in a foul mood, or when he would bash a door or window with such ferocity, the girls would be stunned into silence, their little eyes widening like saucers; fearful of what would happen next.

The answer to my prayer came in the shape of Buddhism. Today I call it my Tina Turner moment because Tina Turner also went through an abusive relationship and used the practice of Buddhism to transform her situation, which she called 'Turning Poison into Medicine.'

Paget did his utmost to isolate me from friends by constantly pointing out their faults regardless of whomever I mentioned. He took to shutting himself away in the bedroom whenever any of them called round, forcing me to stop inviting anyone in, unless I was as sure as I could be, that he would be in a good mood about it.

He and I didn't share the household jobs, so at night I would manage the decorating and cleaning whilst the children slept. Days were filled with caring for their needs until my maternity leave ended, after which I returned to work in addition to engaging an au pair to help me with Nadine and Stephanie.

My second daughter was nearly three years old when I finally realised that my husband would never change and that I would always be in fear of my life if we stayed together. It was a usual family evening in which I was preparing the girls for bed when Paget entered the lounge, vexation written all over his face. He wasn't always like this; sometimes we'd have really good laughs or discussions about affairs of the wider world, but this wasn't one of those times. He was irritated because he couldn't find the car keys. The keys of the car I had purchased on a credit agreement. One of the children had dropped them somewhere and I searched desperately for them, my chest pounding as he got more and more agitated, accusing me of not taking care of things properly. 'Well you should have put them somewhere safely', I retorted. And then I found myself being dragged yet again. The door of the bedroom slammed.

> *My body slammed.*
> *I was a rag doll*
> *I was a nothing.*

I was aware of two innocent and terrified little people in the other room so I kept as quiet as I could so as not to alarm them even further. I heard one call out 'Mummy.' I didn't answer, just took the blows until he'd spent his venomous rage. Finally, I accepted that I was living with someone who only had two settings – zero and 'off the scale.' It took this one more incident of punches, kicks, steps on my throat to realise that I had to leave this relationship before either he killed me – or I killed him.

Seven years after my glorious wedding, I was granted a divorce under the grounds of 'Unreasonable Behaviour.'

Fear and courage walk side by side
Each determining to be in charge.

'It is best that I lead', fear said
'For I am the greatest
and deserve to be spread.'

Track record taught fear that he could certainly win
In the unending struggle between courage and him.

Fear speaks loudly when it comes to stay
In the thoughts and minds of any prey.
Nestling easily with essence of charm
It sits contentedly into willing arms.

But like an unexpected friend
engaging in a battle to surpass and cage,
Courage surges forward to take center stage.

Journey to Love

I was left with a considerable number of negative beliefs about myself because of my childhood abuse. The whole business messed up my head as I got older, and I was never able to reconcile the baggage of uncomfortable feelings that lay dormant inside me. Since my first 'sexual' experience was an exploitation of my body, I grew up with a fundamental belief that I was flawed. I believed it was my fault, sowing a seed of self-hatred because on some level I knew it was wrong. I did not tell anyone about the abuse until I was an adult because he told me not to. I was an obedient seven-year-old you see, who did as I was told by adults in charge of me. I didn't know I had a choice.

Unable to face my inner darkness of unworthiness, anxiety, and a poor self-image; I poured my energies into focusing on external things in my life. I built a successful teaching career, single-handedly raised my two wonderful daughters, and sought love wherever I could find it. When memories of the abuse threatened to surface, I pushed down these painful, tortured moments and worked even harder at things I could control.

Owing to the abuse, I equated love with sex which generated a roller coaster of incompatible relationships. I didn't grow up learning about sex from either of my parents. The closest my mother came to speak to me about it, was when I started my periods. Touching my arm gently, she bent close to my ear and whispered: 'If a man touches Yu, Yu can have a baby.' I was not sure who was more embarrassed, she or me. Even more worrying, when as a family we were grouped around our black and white television and an amorous scene appeared, Dad would be told 'to turn it over.' Hence, I quickly recognised that in my home, sex or anything close to it was off-limits. Thanks to biology lessons at school and conversations with my school friends, I soon learnt the truth. However, in school, we were only given lessons about the physical aspect and nothing about any emotions or feelings that could arise from it.

In my earliest teenage years, a member of the family thought it was okay to show me his privates whenever he visited our home. Under the guise of heading to the bathroom, he would knock the door of bedroom and when I opened it, would proudly reveal his knob, at which I'd withdraw back into the safety of my room. Some years later I found the courage to tell my Mum, but she didn't believe me and laughed. I again tried to reach out for support later in my life because by now my inner self was over-run by disparaging views of myself. Subsequently, I opened up to a close member of my family about being molested as a kid; his response was to remark that 'Yes men who do that are seeking the energy from a child.' I was hoping for a different reaction, like: 'I'm sorry that happened to you', or 'how did you cope?' or 'Is there anything I can do to support you now? No, he merely changed the subject by telling me that he knew women who had experienced much worse; so, I kept on quashing my feelings of anger, powerlessness, and abandonment.

My younger self armed without a road map, set out on a journey of having sexual relations with men hoping against hope to find someone that loved me. I was ever expectant that when I found 'the one'; it would erase all sense of worthlessness that I carried within me, like heavy pieces of luggage you can never let go of.

Following the ending of my marriage, I went in pursuit of my 'prince charming' once more; only to end up with cheaters, scammers, and liars or simply those unwilling to commit to a sincere relationship; all except one. A dear man who I met through my Buddhist community. Although our relationship ended after some years, he inspired me to begin the process of healing from the mistreatment that I had experienced from men in the past.

The cultural values around men in my family were that they came first. We females were expected to be compliant and accommodating without making a fuss. If I deigned to speak my mind the result was either an angry response or the silent treatment, no discussion, just silence. It was like being dismissed because my words were not considered valuable. Men's roles were clear – provider. Women's roles were also clear – housekeeping. I have since acceded that secretly, Mum did not want me to be harnessed by such restraints, hence her pushing me earnestly to get an education.

I had tried all sorts of things to make things different. I wanted to change the dance of meet him, spend good times, fall away into nothingness. I desired a different, happier outcome, but accepting their behaviour in silence didn't work, talking to them didn't change anything, couple counselling didn't work. I even read loads of self-help books in the wish to gain ideas from what others had gone through; but nothing worked long term. In the end I always walked away, more dispirited with each disappointment. Eventually I got my answer – I needed to change! I needed to stop looking for love outside of myself! I began by composing a letter which I will share with you now:

Hey you men,

It has taken all these years later for me to really face and accept what you did to me. Each of you used my body for your own pleasure without a thought about whether it was pleasing me.

Yes, I allowed it – simply because I didn't think I had a choice. I was brought up to believe that my purpose was to please a man, no matter what. No matter that I didn't want to have sex with you. Sometimes it felt like you were merely 'going toilet' in me. You made me feel unworthy. You made me feel as if I was disgusting and had no right to expect any better. Some of you played with my mind, making me believe that I owed you sex because you hadn't had it for a long time, and I was the one who was there.

I was weak, weary and vulnerable; but you didn't see that. You made me feel that all I was good for was great sex, which I gave; all the time becoming a woman who projected sensuality and sex wherever I went; hoping to get my attention that way, because I knew no other.

None of you were ever really interested in how I was feeling inside. You found contentment because I had filled your need – not mine. I needed more and you didn't recognise it; even though I tried to tell you – till I stopped talking; gagged by my own emotions. As each one of you entered and left my life, I used cigarettes to smoke down the agonising feelings. I wish you'd seen that there was more to me than a great shape, firm bum, great legs. None of you got to know my heart. I felt like you saw me as someone to 'tame'; and the way you did it was in the bedroom. And yes, I did enjoy sex with you because I enjoy sex but sex without love and respect, is fruitless, empty, ugly – and that's what you all gave me. Who was worse than whom? I don't know, but it started with you, old man, when I was only a kid – a seven-year-old kid.

Slowly but surely, I transformed all the damaging beliefs that lay hidden in the darkness of my life, into positive ones. I began to deeply appreciate my own needs and ideals, no matter what anyone did or said. I became aware that I had allowed people to criticize, belittle and dismiss my views all in the name of 'I'm only joking,' or 'You're too sensitive'; never open to how hurtful their comments made me feel.

Consequently, I gradually became a woman who values and respects herself from the very core.

Knowing that I deserved better, my relationships have significantly changed as I stepped away from certain people to bring about the amazing woman I really am. Steadily but surely, I climbed the steps of self-value and respect; arriving at a place where the most important person to me was myself - the person I needed to love the most.

My body is precious
My life is precious
My heart is precious
My love is precious.

Jeanette and Liam

After three years of succeeding in the management of the YM, I begun to miss classroom teaching. Choosing a position in which I could continue to impact the lives of young people disillusioned with the education system; I moved into the avenue of special needs - specifically children with behavior and emotional difficulties.

Documentary evidence and my own awareness recognized that for decades a high proportion of black Caribbean, mixed white and black Caribbean students, especially boys were more likely to be identified in the category of behavior, emotional, social, and emotional difficulties than their white counterparts. Research also showed that black students were most susceptible to being placed in Pupil Referral Units or excluded from regular schooling. With this in mind, I returned to the schooling system as an English teacher at a school for excluded pupils in Tottenham, North London.

My heels clicked noisily on the grey pavement whenever I headed to the cabin outbuilding that was my classroom. It stood about 20 meters from the main premises accommodating the other classrooms and the school offices. The students that I taught, were a mixed bunch of urban teenagers.

'Hey. Miss What a we doing today?' Jack shouted, sitting nonchalantly on the side of his desk, one leg swung over the corner's edge.

'I've just told you Jack, but you need to sit at your table properly for us to proceed with the lesson.'

'Why does he have to sit at his table Miss, you know he can't sit still much, pipped up a voice from the other end of the room.'

'Well, in my classroom we all sit down to work because it helps us focus.'

'Do you sit at a table at your house Miss?' exclaimed another voice.

'This isn't about Me Keiron, but since you ask, Yes, I do. It helps me to concentrate properly when planning and marking your work, rather than being scrunched up in my sofa.'

'Well, I know a better way of concentrating Miss', Keiron responded, giving rise to a wave of laughter about the room. Shaking my head with the intention of letting him know I didn't want his answer, he blurted out 'Weed Miss, that would help you concentrate.'

'I can focus good from here Miss', Jack interjected grinning. I could see where the conversation was heading. Most of the students would do anything to delay getting down to any work. Although they showed up for school, it was mostly to meet up with friends and be somewhere safe during the day. Some wanted to learn but didn't have the belief in themselves that they could achieve, and many scarred with enormous emotional hurts made it even harder for them. It was because of my awareness of their emotional issues that prompted me to apply for and obtain a counselling qualification whilst employed at that school.

The skills I learnt from the Counselling Course enabled me to develop an empathetic connection with each student which was particularly useful when one day I was leaving my classroom at break time and nearly tripped over Jeanette, sat perched on the steps outside. To see her head buried in folded arms, her upper body jolting repeatedly, was unusual to say the least. Jeanette was a particularly challenging student, prone to absenteeism who railed against structures of any kind. She fought hard to remain verbally aggressive as much as possible; yet on the odd occasion you would see her tenderly support someone who was upset or engage in helping another student 'get' the work.'

'What's up Jeanette'?

Silence.

'Jeannette I can see you're distressed, what's up'?

'Mind your own business!', she bit back.

I knew not to touch a student who was upset in case it was misinterpreted in anyway. The students distrusted supportive arms or hugs, seeing this type of affection as an assault on their privacy; yet she was clearly painfully upset.

I asked again. 'Has someone upset you Jeannette, you know you can either talk to me or would you like me to take you over to the office where you can sit in the welfare room for a while? I can walk over with you if you like?' Too many questions I realized. I started again.

'Jeannette what's up?' and waited.

The sobs got louder forcing her to blurt, 'Mi Dad's comin outta prison today and it's his birthday and I don't know if I should buy him a card.'

My heart shuddered as I recollected her history of having a father who had murdered her mother and here, she was, a young girl with the dilemma of wanting to do the right thing for her dad, yet with the constant awareness of what he'd done.

This was only one of the challenges I faced in teaching these young people and I learnt to respond as best as I could to each one. The fact that she'd opened up to me was tantamount to the type of person I am, generally calm in nature though strict when needed. Gradually her resistance to my offer of sympathy eased, enabling me to offer reasonable suggestions on what her options could be.

Another of my experiences at this school involved two boys. Alone in my classroom after school, I was putting the final additions to some lesson plans when in walked two lads from my class. I could immediately feel a downturn in energy when they strode into the room. 'Alright boys?' I called out, my stomach stirring uncomfortably as I said it. I was hoping the light tone in my voice would brighten the mood. 'Did you forget something?'

The first boy sauntered closer to me, a smirk on his face. 'Why don't you ever get angry Miss? You never get angry. The second boy brandished a nervous laugh and moved within inches of the first boy. My breath gusty and short, I asked again. 'Did you forget something boys?' Neither replied to my question; instead, the first boy pulled out a knife and started swinging it in my direction. 'Go on Miss get angry' he slapped. 'You're al good and weird. We wanna see you get angry.' Where was the caretaker when I needed him? I considered, while glancing out of the small window to the side of me. The boys stood in jeans and tee-shirts looking innocent; smiles on their faces; at the same time, wafting a putrid scent of confrontation.

My frazzled mind worked hard to focus, to come up with a solution - Should I shout? Should I run? Was anyone in the office in the other building? From somewhere deep inside I heard myself say, 'Look boys you know there are two of you.' Raising the palms of my hands in surrender, and shrugging my shoulders, I continued. 'There's nothing I can do if you choose to harm me.' I kept my voice steady and low yet with a clarity of steel; all the time wearing a fixed smile.

The blade moved nearer to my neck, forcing me to inhale the odorous sweat of its keeper. Repetition is a distinct skill of a good teacher and I used it then. I repeated my initial communication, word for word. Combined with a deranged laughter leaping from his lips, Liam eventually lowered his weaponed arm - a glazed look in his eyes. Turning away from me he ordered his mate to 'Chuh come on.' I dropped to the floor as soon as I saw them stroll out of the door, 'kissing their teeth' as they left.

Liam and James were given long exclusions from the school, and I was filled with the fear of it happening again. I therefore decided to return to mainstream secondary education, with an acute desire to support that system in limiting the number of black students from ending up in Special Schools. I was able to carry this out in my seven-year employment at a North London Secondary School.

I was the only teacher of Caribbean heritage working at the school at that time. In conjunction with my classroom timetable as an English teacher, I introduced a home school initiative. Having evidenced that minority group students, whom were at risk of poor academic achievement, was linked to a division between their home and school; I invested much time and energy into supporting them and their families. I provided clear understanding and knowledge of the English curriculum and the educational system to parents. This enabled them to better support their children with their studies. My system of care led to a new whole school policy, in support of this initiative because I had generated a marked increase in pupil attendance and improved parental cooperation.

Following these successful and rewarding years at Fortismere, my teaching career was interrupted by a near fatal car accident forcing me to leave my job on ill health grounds.

The beautiful rose
Lay dormant and worn.
Closed and beaten by the fiercest of storms
She retreated.

Buddhism

In January 1988 I unexpectedly made a connection with Nichiren Buddhism, whilst attending a writing course at the City Lit College in Central London. When the small group of us were sorting through our folders in preparation for our weekly session, a magazine revealing the word Buddhism on the front cover, fell out of Mandy's folder.

'Are you a Buddhist?' I asked quietly.

'Yes, I am. I can tell you more about it at break if you like?'

'No, you're okay, I'm a Christian.'

'That's alright', she replied pleasantly. There are lots of similarities we can share and'….Mandy wasn't able to continue as the Tutor called for our attention to the day's work.

Our class was on a Monday morning, and I had noticed over the weeks of attending that she just had this nice demure about her which wasn't usual for the rest of us who tended to be more Monday morning bluesy than Monday morning cheery as she was. So, we met for coffee.

Mandy's dark brown hair bobbed around her semi tanned skin making her look almost Moroccan. Whilst seated and holding our hot drinks, we exchanged small details about our backgrounds. We had spoken in class before, so I wasn't completely oblivious to the kind of person she was, but in that moment, I wanted to learn why she'd become a Buddhist. She let me know that through her Practice' as she called it, she had been able to change lots of personal difficulties into joy filled triumphs, just by chanting the words Nam Myoho Renge Kyo.

Mandy relayed how she'd been brought up in a household of alcoholism where she and her siblings hadn't received any positive influences from their parents because of their addiction to alcohol. They were constantly beaten and ridiculed at any given opportunity. She explained how that had left her feeling useless and fearful as she grew into adulthood until she met a woman who introduced her to Buddhism. I was intrigued by the fact that she did not bear a trace of resentment or anger towards her parents when she outlined the scenarios of having to go to bed hungry because her parents spent their money on drink rather than food. Mandy had been practicing, as she called it for ten years when I met her. I wasn't sure why she called it 'practicing' since she seemed to be an expert on Buddhist philosophy. Much later I learnt that the 'practicing' bit referred to the act of chanting the words Nam-Myoho-Renge-Kyo, studying the teachings of Nichiren Daishonin and telling other people about those teachings.

'What does Um MyO Ren thingy mean?' I cut in; puzzlement screened across my face. 'Nam-Myoho-Renge-Kyo' she declared, 'pronounced Nam- Mi oho- Rengay- Cure. Try it with me.'

'No, you tell me how it helps you', I counteracted. Actually, I wasn't comfortable about saying the chanting words again because I knew I couldn't say them the way she had.

Mandy resumed her story, telling me that she'd always wanted to become a writer, but her background limited her self-belief and confidence to go for what she wanted. However, through the chanting she begun to develop an inner confidence leading her to take action by applying for writing jobs on magazines and local newspapers. She stressed that her practice was a practice of 'never giving up'; so, despite some rejection letters she continued her quest by doing a set amount of chanting each day, doing the morning and evening prayers called Gongyo and attending meetings where she could be inspired and inspire others.

'But any faith can do that, except the chanting bit of course.'

'Agreed', she said smiling, moving her coffee cup to the table's edge, and looking at me more intently. The difference with chanting Nam-Myoho Renge-Kyo is that when one chants, one activates the wisest, most compassionate, most courageous part of oneself. 'You see', she stated at the same time, brushing strands of her shoulder length hair from her face. 'Buddhism does not advocate blind faith. Simply explained, Nam-Myoho-Renge-Kyo means, putting our life in rhythm with the universe.

'Uh Uh.' I said, still perplexed.

Aiming to defuse my confusion she changed tact. 'In other words, chanting aligns us with the natural energy that pervades life. It is something that we are all connected to, and this practice brings us into alignment with it – opens our soul to it if you like. Without pausing Mandy continued. I could hear the conviction in her voice as she carried on.' 'We all have within us the ability to overcome any problem or difficulty, and I mean any problem,' she emphasised, perhaps noticing the disbelief shadowing my face. 'It has the capacity to transform any suffering because our inner life is inseparable from the law of life, which is Mystic.' At last, she stopped, opening up a chance for me to enquire how this all helped her to become the writer she wanted be.

'As I said before,' she uttered, less loudly now as she spied the curious glances from across the cafeteria. Mandy was not only vocal with her explanations but simultaneously waved her hands around a lot, as she was speaking. 'Nam-Myoho-Renge-Kyo activates the greatest parts of oneself, so for me, I gained the confidence and determination to go for my dream of working in publishing. With consistent chanting and studying of the teachings, I overcame my feelings of hopelessness leading me to achieve my own column in a national magazine,' she exclaimed, resembling an excited child being given a secretly desired gift.

'Just by chanting the Nam-My O words? I asked suspiciously.

'Yep. Just try it. Test it for yourself.

Warming to her story, I opened up about the life I was living with my husband, to which she listened attentively, expressing no judgement. At the end of my outpouring, she proclaimed that if I chanted the words 'Nam Myoho Renge Kyo', my life would become happy. For some reason I believed her but when I look back, I see that I was so desperate to change the conditions of my marriage that even if she'd said chant the words 'eggs and bacon' at the top of St Paul's cathedral I would have done that too. As it was, she invited me to chant Nam Myoho Renge Kyo to my heart's content.

When we are experiencing our fiercest sufferings, our lives can draw positive influences towards us in the most unforeseen ways - if our hearts are open to it. For me it was my introduction to Nichiren Buddhism. I started to chant on the evening that I met Mandy and have continued ever since. I have now been 'practicing' for 32 years. What drew me to this philosophy of life was the conviction in the teachings that human life has the potential to turn any negative tendency into a force for the creation of good. It is a hope-filled philosophy that goes against a belief in people being born as 'sinners.'

Since meeting Mandy I have become a part of an organisation called the SGI. (Soka Gakkai International). Soka is another name for hope, and Gakkai means value creating society. We as Buddhists meet in each other's homes and purpose-built buildings, to chant, discuss and listen to inspirational guidance on overcoming challenges. (Changes have been made in response to the 2020 pandemic). There is no financial remittance required and all meetings engage a microcosm of society - that is people of all ages, culture, religion, race, economic background and so on. Through this organisation I have acquired an extensive family of like-minded people whose mission in life is to create a peaceful world through one-to one dialogue.

Being raised in a family that frowned upon any negative emotions such as anger, frustration, fear or anxiety, I quickly learnt to bury my own uncomfortable feelings as deeply as possible – and just get on with the 'business of life.' I reasoned quite early on from the words: 'What you crying fa? Stop crying before I give you something to cry about!' meant keep any suggestion of weakness locked up inside. Instead, I was encouraged to admire and center on those things outside of myself. Consequently, I devoted many years to building this idea of valuing and placing considerable emphasis on acquiring external trappings like - academic awards, cars, jobs, houses, romantic relationships, and money. I regarded the pursuit of these as the purpose of my life.

Since practicing Buddhism, I discovered a new message: that

there was nothing wrong with striving for material benefits in and of themselves; but to consider whether each external possession created value for oneself and others simultaneously? Buddhism encourages people to actively contribute value to community, society and the wider world through attitudes and actions.

After the finalisation of my divorce and continual living on an estate that was terribly unpleasant, I sunk into a state of anxiety and depression. Although I maintained my teaching job, I was desperately unhappy at having to live in an environment that was alight with drug use in communal areas. Loud music being played till early hours of the morning and neighbours constantly fighting were also some of issues that got me down. I also wanted my children to attend good schools in a better area. I had no idea how to make the change for us, but I decided to try.

Encouraged by my Buddhist family to chant to make the impossible possible, I set out on a journey to get back on the property ladder. I was thousands of pounds in debt, didn't have any savings and couldn't visualise how to achieve my desire. In the end, I trusted the guidance of those who had 'practiced' longer than I had and begun chanting Nam-Myoho-Renge-Kyo more seriously, to obtain a way out. 'Those who have suffered the most, deserve to be the happiest,' was one such guidance I learnt from Daisaku Ikeda, the leader of the SGI.

Buddhism isn't just about words and prayers; we are inspired to act based on the wisdom that comes up through the chanting. Hence, despite my embarrassment at ending up in my current position, I went to see my bank manager as a first step in getting a new mortgage. Having lost my marital home, it was like starting all over again. He said no and recommended I paid more attention to clearing my debts before entertaining the idea of property ownership again.

I wasn't going to give up though, so I wrote a date in my diary as to when I would achieve my goal. It was to be a year from my visit to the bank. I cut up my credit cards, shopped as frugally as possible and stopped spending on social activities. I chanted consistently about which area would provide the best school for Nadine and Stephanie, an area in which we could feel safe and somewhere accessible to my parents. I also prayed that I would be offered a mortgage that I could afford and would cover the type of home I wanted. Chanting gave me a level of clarity I hadn't known before. I was not receiving any financial support from my ex-husband and therefore needed to develop the courage to 'go it alone.'

Relief from tiredness had to take a back seat as I viewed properties most evenings after work, which was an incredible challenge. When I walked into the three bedroomed house in Roedean Avenue, I knew immediately that it was the right place for us. And when the owners said they could have sold it before but were waiting for the right buyer and how they felt it was me! - I was even more certain. The house and area fulfilled all the criteria I had chanted for.

Throughout the year I received tax rebates, a payout from an old insurance policy and a salary increase 'out of the blue.' Hence, coupled with what I had managed to save, I returned to the bank. The manager was surprised that I had settled such a large debt in such a short space of time. I think he admired my resolve and, on this basis, - I was offered the mortgage.

Just as I started to get comfortable, another obstacle reared its head when I received the invoice from my solicitor. The fees were far greater than I had anticipated, and I didn't have it! I'd worked so hard to get this far and it felt like I was about to fall at the last hurdle. Was it a coincidence that a dear friend called when I was enduring this extremely low point? When I told her what was going on, she promptly offered to lend me the money to pay the solicitor - which I hadn't asked her for! With enormous gratitude to her and to myself for not giving up on my desire, my daughters and I moved into our beautiful new home to begin a new life.

My Sister Bev

My experiences in life have taught me many things, but none as significant as expressed by the words of Arthur Golden in his book 'Memoires of a Geisha'. in which he wrote:

'You cannot read Loss, only feel it'.

My sister was seven when I left home to train as a teacher. These two elements created a distance in our relationship in two ways: firstly, the twelve-year age gap meant I was well past my teens before she'd even entered them, and secondly, my long absences away to follow my teaching Course, fostered my making new friends and new ventures which did not include her.

Bev never really liked herself as much as she liked others. Her friends were important to her, but none were as important to her as her family. She cared and looked up to me. She doted on her nieces, sharing as much of her spare time with them as was possible. I thoroughly enjoyed watching them snigger and chuckle together. Nadine and Stephanie's welfare were something she took seriously, often giving me sound ideas regarding their upbringing.

My sister lived with me for a while when she returned from Jamaica. Knowing of Paget's violent outbursts, prompted her to sleep with a knife under her pillow, ready to attack him if she noticed any ill treatment towards me. I was aware that if it were necessary, she would have given everything she had by fighting with all her might. It helped just knowing she was there, having my back. She was my sister, she had strength. Our living together ended when my parents retuned from Jamaica, and she moved in with them. She also had a special relationship with our brother, leading to her living with him at one point when she was waiting to move into her own flat.

Beverley Jerdine Hylton started her journey in this world in May 1969 as a chubby smiley baby. It was my parent's intention that she was named Beverley Geraldine Hylton, but Mum's mis pronunciation meant her middle name was registered as Jerdine. Bev was Mum and Dad's constant companion and the one that received much attention, leaving my brother and I to form a closer bond as we were closer in age, and therefore had more in common with each other than with a tiny baby. He and I spent our teenage years frequenting the same clubs and dancehalls with our mutual friends; and as we stepped into adulthood it was a familiar picture for family and friends to see us continue this close relationship.

I was in my early twenties when I first acknowledged that my sister intermittently suffered from severe low moods. In trying to make sense of it, my earliest thoughts were that she was overprotected by my parents and therefore didn't have the coping mechanism to function on her own. The first time she took an overdose I was horrified that she could even consider such a thing. I knew she had been self-harming by cutting herself, but this was a new level to me. I remember when she first showed me her arms where she had been cutting herself because she wanted to share with me what she was feeling. But I could barely relate.

I had returned from my teachers' training college for the usual summer break and Beverley showed me the scars; dark lines cascading both sides of her arms like ant trails. 'What are you doing?' I responded angrily, while pushing her outstretched arm away from my eyes. She was couched in her bedroom at my parents' home in Duke Street. She couldn't give me a reason that I could get my head around; answering that it just made her feel better afterwards. I was stunned into silence, my mind questioning: How could someone feel better after deliberately cutting them self like that? How often had she done it? Was she doing it in her room, when the rest of us were out of the way, watching television perhaps?

On this occasion Mum and Dad were out somewhere, at work I think so it was just the two of us. She was lying on her floral bed cover, legs spread out in front of her, crossed at the ankles. Looking directly into her eyes, I asked again. Why?

Shoulders shrugging, she retorted icily, obviously sensing my lack of empathy.

'I just told you, I don't know. It makes me feel better that's all.' Not knowing what to say or do, I stood watching her hoist one leg over the other as she made her way off the side of the bed. Annoyed, I then did know what to say - and vehemently expressed how I felt she was being selfish and irresponsible both to herself and Mum and Dad. 'You need more counselling!' I exclaimed; slowing down to a more controlled tone as I touched her shoulder. 'Bev, you don't have to do that.' Your life's not that bad. Look at all that you have around you — lovely home, Mum, Dad, me, Winston, your friends. Don't we matter?' Words tumbled from me at varying pitches as she stormed out of the room.

As I tell this story, I am reminded that I had to relive a similar situation with my youngest daughter, when she too began to self-harm by cutting her arms during her teens.

Bev continued to self- harm and undertook further overdoses; one clashing with the same time that my brother developed cancer, warranting an emergency operation prior to treatment. Without warning, I found myself in the position of having both my siblings in hospital at the same time; one fighting for his life, the other slowing it down.

I was left to support the anguish of my parents, maintain a full-time teaching job and take care of my two young children as a single Mum. It was a time in my life when I experienced the worst kind of internal agony yet managed to 'keep all the balls in the air', with a strength I never knew I had.

I used my chanting and study of Buddhism to deepen my understanding of why my brother and sister had to experience such major health trials in their life. I chanted with every ounce of my being that they would both fully recover as quickly as possible. I prayed that they both had the strength to overcome their illnesses and that my parents would be strong enough to bear the pain they were undergoing.

After coming through his operation, my brother begun a seemingly incessant chemotherapy treatment where his body was locked into a cycle of painful needles, fatigue, infections, nausea, hair and weight loss, fertility problems and much more. Eventually however, he managed to recuperate from the potent disease that could have ended his life. In due course, Beverley also overcame her situation following her successful health treatment at the Homerton Hospital in East London.

My father used to help with the maintenance of my garden

in Roedean Avenue, Enfield. At nearly 100ft, I couldn't manage it alongside the care of Nadine, Stephanie and full-time work, so his assistance was invaluable. Dad would always arrive with his bag of gardening clothes and tools, ever eager to tackle the weeding and 'dig up the groan' (ground)' as he liked to say. On November 9th, 2000, he was different. Unlike his usual sparky self, he was agitated. Every half hour or so he would remark that neither he nor Mum had heard from Bev all day, which was unusual. My constant reassurance that Bev would be in touch when she was ready only appeased him in short bursts. Though I insisted that she was probably sleeping or chatting to her friends and would call them later, his worry barely faltered. 'Yes, it must be so it go', and would quickly return to concern.

As he scraped and raked, I made greater attempts at keeping him calm, by providing copious cups of tea with bun and cheese, one of his favourite snacks, until it was time for him to leave. At around 6 o clock, head hung low, he Mumbled, 'I ope nuttin nuh appen to ar', (hope nothing has happened to her), just before I closed the main door behind him. There wasn't any need for any discussion between us - I knew what he meant as he said it. When he got home, the first thing Dad did was to ask my Mum whether she'd heard from Bev to which she worriedly responded with a 'No. I wonder where she is?' and then called me to check whether I'd heard from my sister. More reassurance was given, though less convincingly.

At that time Bev was no longer living a few roads away from my parents but had moved into an assisted living premises for those with mental health difficulties, in West London. Winston and I didn't think it was the best solution for her problems but armed with the same strength of character of our family, Bev insisted this was where she wanted to be and collaborated hard with the local authorities to be granted a place. In less than 1 year of having moved there, she was dead. At around 8 o clock that evening the phone rang with the harrowing news. Sharing the same family values, my dearest sister had almost too much emotion but nowhere to go with it until they imploded within her, and she took her life by filling her body with excess insulin at the age of thirty-one.

It was as if someone had thumped me hard in my stomach - and kept on thumping; thump, thump, thump; my chest tightening as I looked from Mum to Dad; both staring at me with disbelief as I relayed the telephone conversation from the police; before crumbling towards the floor and each other in slow motion.

Similar to my brother and myself, Bev adored reading. Her bookshelves were stacked with an assortment of subjects including science, self-help, fiction novels and books about learning effectively. Bev attended the same Secondary School as I had, prior to completing her Secondary education in Jamaica. Sadly, she had to contend with being compared to her 'big sister' by the teachers. I don't agree with this attitude because I believe that all children should be treated as individuals and not be compared with anyone, as this can lessen that child's awareness of their own uniqueness and personal growth. Sometimes we just cannot do anything about how people behave, but for Bev it was kind a cool knowing she had met the staff who had taught me. After returning to England, she went on to take several adult Education courses to continue her love of learning.

Beverley's trademark was her jewellery, and only gold would do – hooped earrings, bangles, rings galore, you name it, she had it. Whether she was dressed in leggings and baggy top or a fashionable long skirt and top; her neck, wrists and earlobes were always suitably glinted. My good fortune was being able to borrow from a very choice selection. Bev was also a music fan, not especially the heavy drum and bass reggae that my brother and I liked, but more mellowly stuff, such as Lovers Rock and some easy listening jazz compilations. Her interest in medicine prompted her to commit to voluntary work with the St John's ambulance service for several years; and being an advocate of medical research, she also participated in some clinical trials.

One of my fortuitous experiences spent with Bev, was when she, I, and a cousin of ours, went to Amsterdam for a weekend. We'd been planning it for weeks and Beverley being the organized person she was, excitedly took pains to show me pictures of places that we 'had' to see. Three of them being, the beach, the Anne Frank house, and the famed canals. In the clear waters of Amsterdam's beach resort, Bev embraced the blazing sunlight contouring against her smooth dark skin. Hair plaited in cane rows arranged neatly to the back of her neckline, she enjoyed paddling among equally chirpy holidaymakers. The three of us relished the scenes of the prominent waterways and I relished the time I had with my eleven-year-old sister.

Bev started working with special needs children in her early twenties. She thoroughly enjoyed boating with them along the English coasts of southern England during their school breaks. Smiling contentedly, she preferred to relax on the stern end of the rowing boat leaving the steering to her colleague. On these trips away with the boisterous children, Bev fully busied herself with arts and craft activities, totally throwing herself into playing and intermingling with them. Undeterred by camping out in tents without home comforts, Beverley would hug, support, laugh with the racial blend of primary aged children around her; only separating herself to photograph special moments.

Buried within the veins of my heart you sit contentedly.

Each strand of your life secreted across we trio of Hylton siblings

Versatility spanned all endeavours that you undertook, pulsing care towards all that entered your sights.

Engaged in a struggle of anguish drumming at your soul you fought hard,

Richer in wisdom to know who you were and when you would complete your earth journey then

Leaving your body to wander free to teach me that life can be a land of hope – not hopelessness

Even greater through your passing of time.

You began an early path towards the unknown, showing me that death is real, death is not to be feared, death means a new life – and I thank you.

Tribute to my Father

Dad was a principled man who led by example. Lester Hylton arrived in England from Jamaica aged 25. His father, Angel Hylton encouraged him to leave the toil of working as a land cultivator in Jamaica. 'Sey buoy, Yu waan go a inglan?' my grandfather announced after he'd heard that England was offering the opportunity to West Indians to work in the 'mother country.' Not knowing what to expect but seeing a chance to improve his way of life and trusting his father's guidance, my father headed towards his future. Lester was one of 11 children, him being the third eldest of all his siblings but the eldest of those who travelled and came to live in England.

Lester worked on the assembly line at the Fords Motor Company for most of his life before coming up to retirement, after which he obtained a part time position as a security guard, at a clinic in his local area. At Fords, his hours were divided into shifts which rarely matched up with when the rest of our family were free to socialise or sleep. However much he wished this were different, his staunch commitment to working practices took precedence. Lester Hylton often returned home from his shift work in neatly pressed dark blue overalls, carrying with him the scent of hard toil and engine grease. He loved his job, regarding it as a constructive way to support his family. His drive to maintain our life in a 'bought' house was remarkable, considering the low wage he was receiving. He used to say, 'Me no want oonu grow up in a tenant house.'

Dad drove a navy-blue ford Cortina car which he took considerable pride in; ensuring it was cleaned and polished on a weekly basis. Shortly after passing taking driving lessons, I borrowed his car with his knowledge to go and meet friends. However, I drove too fast and too close to a nearby car, causing a serious dent on the rear right-side door. My Dad had trusted me to drive his precious jewel after a large dose of begging and pleading - and then this happened! Fearfully, I parked the car someway from the house when I returned home, despite knowing that he was due to go to work that night and would therefore see it within hours. I was trying to think of what to say about the accident, becoming excessively afraid of his response.

I was too nervous to say anything when I went in and instead went straight to my room to read; quietly awaiting the moment he'd walk out of the house. The moment arrived and his footsteps sounded louder than usual. In what seemed no time at all, I was alerted to the sound of his key re-entering and turning the lock of the main door of our home. My heart pumped unrhythmically as he called my name. 'Yes Daddy.' I called back.

'Come ere.'

My steps were slower than usual as I ambled towards the front door where he was still standing. 'Yes Daddy', I repeated nervously; quickly reading his face for signs of anger.

Dad proceeded to question me about the dent that he'd seen on the car and after listening to my stammered account of how it happened, he laughed. And laughed again with that boisterous spirited laugh that he had - mid giving me a description of his own first accident. Then gently patting my shoulders he announced his joy at my being safe and unhurt. When I least expected it, he had displayed the mild side of his nature. As a devoted father, he delighted in ensuring that there was always enough food on the table. I cannot remember there never being anything to eat. Sometimes the foods were a little scarce and we'd turn our noses up at corned beef and rice – again! My favourite was his peas soup on a Saturday and even when I was living away from home, he would still ring me during the week and tell me that he had prepared soup for me to come and collect for myself and the girls. He was a man who would cook most days except Fridays when we would be treated to fish and chips.

During his retirement years, Dad made himself available to help in my garden alongside tending to his allotment. He owned a large metal knife, which he used for gardening, for as long as I can remember. Like everything in his life that he cared for, Dad's agricultural tools were no exception. At the start of every usage, they sat, displaying the shine and polished handling he had given to them.

Brandishing a tired looking bucket shaped hat on his head, he would de bud young flowers along with the weeds in my garden. He just wasn't very good at discerning the difference between either plant; so dressed in paint and grass-stained dark trousers with turn ups, supported at his waist by a weather worn brown belt tightly fastened above his waist; Dad would unceremoniously cut down any stemmed leaves that showed any hint of colour. It made me snigger as I assessed whether the flowering shoots were displeased at having placed a lot of energy into growth, only to be stunted by my Dad's enthusiastic gardening - with his shiny machete knife. Lester Hylton was a stickler for timekeeping, whilst the members of his family were not. Whenever there was a planned family outing, Dad would be ready, hat and coat in hand, often several hours before the designated time of departure. I joked with him once or twice when he was due to travel abroad, that, 'It's too early Dad. Are you trying to get there before even the people who work at the airport, reach?'

Dad's laughter amused himself as much as whoever was with him. His semi bald head would ease forward as he shared a comment which he considered hilarious. No one could help laughing or smiling along with him even if what he said wasn't especially funny. The corner of his eyes would sparkle playfully whenever he watched his eldest granddaughter as a toddler, dance 'of a fashion', to the theme tune of his weekly soap opera. And when his beloved West Indian cricketers won a match, he absolutely throbbed with smug grins; anyone would think that he himself had trained the team.

My father was known as Daddy to me, my brother and my sister. I recall him wearing a navy waterproof jacket – when he was old. It hung silently and ceremoniously on a hook next to my Mum's brown one. Side by side they hung in the alcove of their narrow hallway, both waiting for the next outing. Dad would disappear and reappear in the living room zipping up the front of his jacket as he shuffled towards my Mum, repeating the question 'What u want a street Miney?'

'Nothing,' was the customary reply, followed by 'Anyting you see fa me jus buy it.' And then he would look eagerly towards the corner of the room where his lonely walking stick stood. 'You have Yu glasses? Yu have u money? Bring me back Pattie,'

Mum would shout at his disappearing back, the clunk of the closing door and his contented smile.

It was wonderful to see my father lose his rigidity around his relationship with my mother. I was able to experience the eventual high regard he held towards her, as they shared their journey of life together. They had weathered the storms of their early marriage and I applaud both he and my Mum for transforming their marital relationship from one of volatile disharmony into one of the most amusing, loving, respect worthy relationships, I have ever seen.

Dad's shoulders drooped as he ventured into his senior years; yet no lines contoured his face, and following retirement, he kept active by taking a walk every day. His neighbouring retail food sellers on Tottenham high road looked forward to his laugh as he chose his green bananas, or Jamaican sweet potatoes. He and his 'push basket', as he called it, would trundle along collecting the week's groceries from these preferred shops. I enjoyed watching him lift and check each vegetable for signs of decay, putting it sharply back if there was an ounce of decay. He liked the big tomatoes. Daddy liked big things – even the chicken pieces that he bought had to be exceptionally large; he wasn't interested in the slimmer versions found in supermarket chain stores.

I would meet him at his home on a regular basis and off we'd go, him chatting easily about his day thus far. 'Me win the bingo', he said once.

'That's good Daddy' I'd reply.

'Yes, me win 50 pone (pound) and me goin to share it with you and dem girls and Winston.' Whatever Dad won on the lottery or bingo sheets from his tabloid newspaper, he would share. He also split any winnings he gained from horse betting which wasn't something he did often but liked to give me detailed explanation about who rode, who nearly won and what each-way meant. I simply feigned interest yet took pleasure in his ramblings. He was ever hopeful of winning enough money 'to help oonuu out.'

Dad was a church goer who rarely missed attending his local Baptist congregation, often sharing stories of who hadn't shown up, what the sermon was about and what aspects of the sermon that he enjoyed. Lester's long-standing Christian beliefs did not stop him supporting my Buddhist faith. On one occasion he willingly accompanied my daughters and myself to the central Buddhist Centre in Taplow Court, Berkshire.

Practicing Nichiren Buddhism led me to a new understanding of life and death, especially following the death of my sister. It was suggested to me that until one understood death, one couldn't properly experience the joy of life. I took it to mean that until we face the inevitability of death, then somewhere deep within our life we would always be afraid of it. I considered whether people who had been exposed to 'near death' experiences lost their fear around the whole subject but couldn't come up with a definitive answer because I had only met a handful of people who had undergone such an occurrence. I mused about what happens after death; having been raised and educated to believe that after death, 'good' people went to heaven and 'bad' people went to hell. That idea didn't sit well with me as what was good and what was bad was too open to a range of interpretations, so I delved deeper and explored Buddhist viewpoints.

Buddhism supports the notion that life and death are not

independent of each other, but a continuity that persists eternally. It teaches that at the point of death, all positive and negative actions, referred to as karma; shape the circumstances in which lives become manifest again through birth, as a new individual life. Not the same as the Christian concept of an individual's soul living eternally in either hell or heaven; rather that when someone dies it is because the person has completed his or her purpose and at the right time, will appear again – and this cycle continues.

In my opinion, the ultimate questions of life and death are in the end, a matter of theory and belief. Since death is inescapable, I conclude that what truly counts is:

Are we making positive or negative actions in our life?

Are we aware of the preciousness of life?

and what value are we creating whilst we are living?

Fear of death sprung from the shadows of my mind when I encountered the serious illnesses of my immediate and extended family members; and especially when I suffered a major car accident, from which I escaped alive but underwent severe physical and emotional struggles as a result. However, any understanding about death I had gained from my searches, did not prepare me for the assault of grief which descended on me, at the death of my father.

'No sign of life.' These were the words I read about my Dad as he lay in a stillness I wasn't used to. Even though the four words were clearly written on his death certificate; I found it hard to comprehend the meaning, despite having witnessed his lifeless body first-hand. - Like a silent thief, death had grabbed him away, penetrating his heart.

Following an inexpressibly painful time of grief, I decided

that it doesn't matter what one believes happens after death, but whether one can eventually feel at peace after the grief has eased. My father's death taught me the importance of living a life of no regrets – fully savoring the joys of each given moment. Dad left me with strong moral values and standards; but none more treasured than his insistence that:

'What is right for you Rose, will never pass you by.'

Lester Hylton
Born October 16. 1931
Departed peacefully 4th November 2013

Tribute to Mum

One of the greatest gifts given to me by my mother was her insistence in my getting an education. She told me several times to 'Get Yu education because nobody can take it from you. Don't bother about Man. Yu education is more important.' Both she and my Dad were extremely elated when I completed my degree. To her, my achievement would stand me in good stead for my future. Mum beamed from ear to ear at my graduation in her brown floral frock, neat as always and clutching her black shiny handbag.

My Mother, Wilhelmina Hylton (nee Richards), was born in Saint Ann's Jamaica in April 1933. In our family it wasn't unusual to be given a name at birth and then called something else throughout your life. In Mummy's case she was christened Wilhelmina but more often referred to as auntie Wilhel, Miney or Miss Miney by friends and family.

One of ten children, Mum was the daughter of Emanuel and Ancella Richards and attended the Gibraltar Elementary school where she begun a dressmaking programme. Her Course ended when she emigrated to England with her older sister Gladys, at the age of twenty-two. She married my father on her birthday in 1956 and started her family a year later.

The general attitude of the British public towards people arriving from the West Indies at that time was hostile. Despite being invited to enter England to support the country's workforce shortage, many Jamaicans like my Mum had to face the distress of racial discrimination in the job and housing market. Fear and anxiety were two conditions she had to cope with in a country that belittled her rights simply because of her skin colour. This was made especially worse as her own mother had died within days of her arrival. In testament to her pluckiness, Mum worked hard alongside my father to buy their own property and provide my siblings and I with the best care possible.

Mum was a hardworking person who preferred to look after her children herself; so, when she arrived in England she worked as a machinist so that she could be at home for us. When we were old enough, she went out to work as a care assistant. She was also a devoted Christian woman who was baptized in her teens at Gibraltar Baptist Church in Jamaica. From then she, in her words – 'gave herself to the Lord.' Her solid Christian values served as the strength she used to overcome many difficulties in her life. Very few people could enter our Mum's home without being told to 'pray to the Lord'; whether they wanted to hear it or not! She never doubted in the least whether she would be helped by her faith; and strove with a certainty that 'God knows best.' I credit my spiritual strength to my Mum even though we practiced different beliefs. I see now that I have acquired her invaluable attributes of fortitude, insight, and kind-heartedness.

My mother was overweight. Much as she did her best to control her diet, she found it hard to resist foods like sweet potatoes or mouth-watering fried snapper fish and dumplings. It was therefore to her credit that she took part in a 5K Race for Life event. Panting and often out of breath, this woman in her late sixties, wearing jogging pants and tee-shirt fulfilled her desire to 'walk for Bev.' It was the longest she had ever walked, and I was awash with emotion as I watched her gratefully accept her medal and pink sash.

Mum was immensely proud of her children and grandchildren. She often remarked to anyone who would listen, that Nadine and Stephanie 'come out good.' Being a generous woman, she didn't just think about herself but about others too. One of her traits was to give away small gifts of money. She would do this by scrunching a note or two in the palm of her hand, then handing it to whoever she chose - at the same time telling the person, 'Tek dis an buy someting for yuself.' Loving the joy of giving, Mum's brown plump cheeks easily rose and fell as her smile brightened her face.

Mum and I grew closer and closer as the years tipped away from us. When her health issues became chronic, leading to her living in a care home, I was able to share craft and gentle exercise activities with her, which often left us roaring with laughter at the sight of our results. Mum liked to tell me all about the comings and goings of the occupants. Leaning in, she would whisper a detailed tale of who visited whom and how disgusted she was at the infrequent visits from certain family members of some of the residents.

In March 2016 I awoke to see that my mobile had several missed messages from the hospital, which had admitted my mother only days before. My fingers shook as I sought the green connect button. I pressed. It was answered immediately. My heart pounded, desperately trying to escape from my chest.

'Hello, I've just noticed a few calls from you. Is it about my Mum?' I stuttered.

'Yes'

' Is that Rose Hylton'

'Yes'

'I'm afraid your Mum is really ill now.'

The 'now' echoed brutally - Now Now Now…...

'What do you mean? 'But she ate the food I brought to her last night, I rambled, she can't be going…..'

'You need to come now.' Almost hollering, the caller repeated the request. 'There's not much time.' Despite hearing the urgency in her voice, I chattered on. 'Why didn't you ring my landline number?' I replied, unable to stop the tremor and annoyance in my voice; I don't sleep with my mobile next to my bed!' In that instant I wanted her to stop talking even though I was asking her a question. I didn't want to hear anymore.

'Have you called my brother?' I asked with less irritation; to which she answered that she hadn't because I was listed as the primary caregiver.

'You need to come now,' she insisted.

My phone trembled as I delivered the news to my brother and my girls. Despite Winston landing at my house in a flash and driving us to the North Middlesex Hospital as fast as he could; we were too late. The woman who had borne us, loved, and nurtured us, had gone.

Mother dear It's time to rest.

You tried your hardest

You did your best.

Look at the results of the seeds you have sown

Your children and grandchildren all full grown.

We will miss your laughter and your serious face

We will miss the way you took pride of place.

Thank you for the love - that you gave

Thanks for showing us that a woman can be brave.

Sleep well dear mother - your work is done

Your beautiful life can now move on.

Final Thoughts

When I arrived in this world, there was no way of knowing what my journey ahead would look like. As I reflect on my past, I am astounded at the trials I have overcome. There were many times when others let me down and disappointed me. There were numerous occasions when I felt betrayed by others and wanted to give up – roll over and die. At other times I didn't know what to believe in as the onslaughts of trauma took shape over and over again. I smoked too much, I raged at the world, I dated the wrong guys; all to suppress the emotional hurts that lay within.

But a fractured spirit cannot heal until it is brought out into the light, clearly examined, felt and freed. In the wake of a painful acceptance that my life was not flowing in a positive direction, I finally took the last couple of years to dig deep; to face all what I term the dark elements inside, that had haunted me for nearly six decades. It has taken a lot of courage to share some details of my younger years, and today I applaud myself for doing it.

I am currently living in a 'bought' house in Hertfordshire, working as a writer and English tutor. I continue to share blissful moments with the two brightest constants in my life – Nadine and Stephanie. Each has fared well in their professional careers, yet none touches me more than observing their compassionate, courageous, and wise natures. I am also blessed to have a beautiful grand-daughter, Deanna, whose story will be different; yet she will inherit mine and her mother's strength and pluckiness, to also live a remarkable life.

As a result of my experiences, I learnt that I was strong and resilient; I learnt that my accomplishments in my work with young people, rose out of my own multiple traumas. It became my mission, for instinctively I was able to encourage and teach young people - to be the authors of their own lives. I taught them to become the absolute best that they could be - irrespective of their background, class, or social economics. I became grateful for the challenges I met, for without facing our own 'darkness' we cannot truly experience the full joy of living.

Finally, I appreciate that I did my best at every given moment - and that's all any of us can do.

What do you see when you stand in front of yourself?
Can you picture an inside glow of beauty and worthiness?

What do you see when you stand beside the people closest
to you?
Do you feel free and at ease?

What do you see when you walk shoulder to shoulder with
your mate?
Do you see love and affection?
Or do you see competition and strife?

What do you see when you stand in front of yourself?
Do you see the uniqueness of your smile?
Or shadows of gloom seeking to steal the joys from your
heart.

What do you see when you stand in front of yourself?
I hope you constantly see the best in you.

Printed in Great Britain
by Amazon

86007696R00068